PROVERBS

Everlasting Wisdom for Everyday Life

VANCE PITMAN

Lifeway Press®
Brentwood, Tennessee

EDITORIAL TEAM

Cynthia Hopkins
Writer

Reid Patton
Senior Editor

Angel Prohaska
Associate Editor

Jon Rodda
Art Director

Tyler Quillet
Managing Editor

Joel Polk
Publisher, Small Group Publishing

Brian Daniel
Director, Adult Ministry Publishing

2022 Lifeway Press® · © 2022 Vance Pitman

ISBN: 978-1-0877-7177-9
Item number: 005839200

Dewey decimal classification: 223.7

Subject heading: BIBLE. O.T. PROVERBS / WISDOM / GOD--WISDOM

Unless indicated otherwise, all Scripture quotations are taken from the Christian Standard Bible®, Copyright © 2017 by Holman Bible Publishers. Used by permission. Christian Standard Bible® and CSB® are federally registered trademarks of Holman Bible Publishers.

To order additional copies of this resource, write to Lifeway Resources Customer Service; 200 Powell Place, Suite 100; Brentwood, TN 37027; fax 615-251-5933; call toll free 800-458-2772; order online at *lifeway.com;* email *orderentry@lifeway.com.*

Printed in the United States of America

Adult Ministry Publishing • Lifeway Resources • 200 Powell Place, Suite 100 • Brentwood, TN 37027

Contents

About the Author 5

How to Use This Study 6

Interpreting Proverbs 9

WEEK 1

Pursuing Wisdom 10

Proverbs 1–7 16–29

WEEK 2

Receiving Wisdom from the Word 30

Proverbs 8–14 36–49

WEEK 3

Growing in Wisdom Through Relationships . . . 50

Proverbs 15–21 56–69

WEEK 4

Walking in Wisdom Through Life 70

Proverbs 22–31 76–95

About the Author

Vance responded to God's call to Las Vegas, Nevada in 2000, as a church plant sent out from First Baptist Church in Woodstock, Georgia. From a small group of eighteen adults in a living room, Hope Church grew to become a thriving multi-ethnic, multi-generational fellowship of over four thousand members who, today, speak more than fifty languages and who have in common the singular desire to connect people to live the life of a Jesus follower. Vance led Hope to understand that what God is doing is bigger than one church. Since its launch in 2001, Hope has sent hundreds out of its fellowship on mission, invested millions of dollars in God's global activity, and has commissioned more than seventy-five churches in the western United States.

As a seasoned church planter in the West, Vance speaks across the country and all over the world from the passion of his apostolic heart to inspire people to join in God's eternal, redemptive mission of making disciples and multiplying the church among every tribe, tongue, people, and nation. In March of 2022, Vance assumed the role of President of SEND Network, the largest church planting organization in North America, and with it, the role of Senior Vice President of the North American Mission Board.

Vance holds a bachelor's degree with a major in history and a minor in business management from the University of North Alabama, and a master's degree in divinity from Mid-America Baptist Theological Seminary. He resides in Henderson, Nevada, with his wife Kristie. They are the proud parents of four, and have two grandchildren.

PROVERBS

How to Use this Study

This Bible study book includes four weeks
of content for group or individual study.

Personal Study

Each week includes seven to ten proverbs for daily reading and personal study. These studies are meant to cultivate daily time in the Word and a regular practice of reading Proverbs. Each day of personal study has a chapter of Proverbs printed in the book along with a page of devotional content and reflection questions. The Scripture is printed so that you can underline, highlight, and interact with the day's reading.

In this study, Vance Pitman challenges you to join him in reading a proverb a day—reading the proverb that corresponds with the day of the month. If you begin the study in the middle of a month, you can either follow the book or follow the calendar (the personal studies do not have to be read in a particular order.)

Additionally, each day of personal study has a short (one to two minute) video to view on the chapter of Proverbs being covered that day. These short videos are available through Lifeway's On Demand platform. Instructions on how to view all the video content for this study are included on the printed instructions in the back of this book.

Group Sessions

Each week includes a personal study guide that provides questions and directions for group members and group leaders participating in this study. Each group session uses the following format to facilitate simple yet meaningful interaction among group members and with God's Word.

START. This section includes questions to get the conversation started and to introduce the main topic of the session teaching.

WATCH. This section provides space to take notes during the weekly video session. All group videos are included with the purchase of this book through Lifeway's OnDemand platform. Instructions on how to view all the video content for this study are included on the printed instructions inside the backcover of this book.

DISCUSS. This section includes questions and statements that guide the group to explore relevant biblical truth and apply what they've studied over the previous week as they've interacted with the personal studies.

Considerations for This Study

This study on Proverbs can be used in a variety of ways. There are four group sessions and thirty-one days of study. Before using the study you will want to determine how you plan to use it.

AS AN INDIVIDUAL Though this is a group Bible study, all video content is included with the purchase of this book; therefore, this study can be done as an individual. In this case, one would want to start the study at the beginning of the month and go through the study sequentially.

AS A GROUP STARTING AT THE BEGINNING OF A MONTH. Ideally, groups would begin this study at the start of a month and go through the group material each week as they meet together. Throughout this resource, the group sessions occur every seven days, but groups can use them sequentially as they meet throughout the month.

AS A GROUP STARTING IN THE MIDDLE OF THE MONTH. If your group begins this study in the middle of a month you can either start from the beginning and work through the thirty-one days of content, or you can start at the day of the month you begin and go through the group in order. The group content is not directly tied to the daily individual content, so either approach will work.

Interpreting Proverbs

The purpose of the book of Proverbs is to give wisdom to God's people. In Proverbs 1:2, Solomon puts it this way: "for learning wisdom and discipline." But it's important to know more than just the purpose of the book. In order to benefit from the intended purpose, we also have to understand how to read Proverbs.

A good place to begin is by asking, what is a proverb? Proverbs are not exclusive to the Bible, though the types of proverbs found in the book of Proverbs are unique in their nature. In general, a proverb can be defined as a brief but powerful saying that states a general truth. Proverbs are not to be understood as absolute and specific promises of truth. Instead, they express general principles that prove true in most cases.

The proverbs found in the book of Proverbs are unique in that they have been given by God. This gives us certainty of their benefits. Further, the wisdom found in Proverbs is not only beneficial in daily life but also guides us toward eternal life with God. Throughout the book of Proverbs, Solomon exhorts his readers to pursue wisdom over foolishness. As we pursue the wisdom found in this book, we can be confident in its benefits for our lives today and even more so of their eternal value. As Vance reminds us, "Proverbs provides everlasting wisdom for everyday life."[1]

1. Paraphrased from the *CSB Study Bible* intro to Proverbs

WEEK ONE

Pursuing Wisdom

PROVERBS 1-7

Wisdom's Necessity

Every day, all people face situations that invite them to choose from one of two options—wisdom or foolishness. You might not have ever thought about it that way, but it's no less true. In every time and culture, marriage, parenting, friendship, work, and relationships have presented opportunities for unwise thoughts, words, and behaviors. Add the continual redefining of those relationships in our day and time, and those opportunities increase exponentially.

The problem is, we don't often know what is the wise thing to think, say, or do. We may think we know. Have you ever thought you knew the right thing to say or do only to later discover you were wrong? We've all been there! It happens in every area of our lives. We need wisdom for our thoughts, words, earthly relationships, decision-making, life "in" the world, and walk with the Lord.

Ephesians 5:15-17 puts it this way: "Pay careful attention, then, to how you walk—not as unwise people but as wise—making the most of the time, because the days are evil. So don't be foolish, but understand what the Lord's will is." It is not only life experience that shows us we need wisdom. God Himself speaks that truth into our lives. Gratefully, though, God doesn't only tell us to walk in wisdom, He has given us His Word to teach us how.

The book of Proverbs, specifically, offers everlasting wisdom for everyday life. It helps us see life from God's perspective. It aims to help us acquire and apply God's wisdom to the decisions and activities of everyday life at every stage of life. That's why this study encourages us to read through the book of Proverbs, one chapter each day. We need God's wisdom, and Proverbs gives that wisdom to us.

Are you ready?

Start

Use this page to introduce the idea and then get the conversation started.

Proverbs is a book that invites us to find and embrace wisdom. The primary way it does this is by comparing wisdom with what the Bible calls "foolishness." Since wisdom is a word that means different things to different people, let's think through this together.

How would you finish the following sentences?

A person who is wise . . .

A person who is foolish . . .

What are some situations in your life when you knew you needed guidance? Where did you turn to find the answers you were looking for? Why?

Everyday we find ourselves in situations that require wisdom. We need wisdom for everyday life. Thankfully, there's a book of the Bible where God invites us to tap into His wisdom—the book of Proverbs. Throughout this study, we'll walk through the book of Proverbs, discovering together how to see life from God's perspective.

Prayer

Thank God for the gift of His Word. Acknowledge your need for His everlasting wisdom in everyday life. Invite Him to fill you with that wisdom as you pursue Him in your study of Proverbs.

Watch

Use this page to take notes as you watch the group teaching session.

To access the teaching sessions,
use the instructions in the back
of your Bible study book.

Discuss

Use this section to discuss the video teaching.

Vance said, "The Bible is as relevant as the times we are living in." Why do some people struggle to believe that is true? Have you ever questioned whether or not the Bible is relevant in your own life? Explain.

In the gold rush of the 1800s, people left everything behind to mine out treasure—to find gold. How does that serve as a picture of what God intends for us in relationship to His everlasting wisdom? What does it require of you?

Vance explained, "Wisdom is seeing life from God's perspective."
Read Ephesians 5:15-17. Why do we all need God's perspective?

Read Proverbs 1:7. Solomon's words here infer that we have two choices regarding God's Word. What are they? What attitude do you need to receive everlasting wisdom for everyday life? Why?

Read Proverbs 1:1-6. What "everyday life" outcomes will you receive in pursuing God's wisdom?

How is it that Proverbs can provide wisdom in every stage of life (vv. 4-5)?

Vance gave a sampling of wisdom in Proverbs related to the following areas of life—your relationship with God, your relationships with others, decision-making, and the words we speak. In which of these areas of life do you currently sense the most need for wisdom? Why?

Vance has challenged us to, each day, read the chapter in Proverbs that corresponds with the day of the month. What wisdom do you hope to glean as you join in that journey?

Close the group in prayer and remind them to complete the week's personal study.

MONTH   DAY   YEAR

THE PURPOSE OF PROVERBS

1 The proverbs of Solomon
    son of David, king of Israel:
2 For learning wisdom and discipline;
    for understanding insightful sayings;
3 for receiving prudent instruction
    in righteousness, justice,
    and integrity;
4 for teaching shrewdness
    to the inexperienced,
    knowledge and discretion
    to a young man—
5 let a wise person listen
    and increase learning,
    and let a discerning person
    obtain guidance—
6 for understanding a proverb
    or a parable,
    the words of the wise,
    and their riddles.

7 The fear of the LORD
    is the beginning of knowledge;
    fools despise wisdom and discipline.

AVOID THE PATH OF THE VIOLENT

8 Listen, my son,
    to your father's instruction,
    and don't reject
    your mother's teaching,
9 for they will be a garland of favor
    on your head
    and pendants around your neck.
10 My son, if sinners entice you,
    don't be persuaded.
11 If they say— "Come with us!
    Let's set an ambush
    and kill someone.
    Let's attack some innocent person
    just for fun!
12 Let's swallow them alive, like Sheol,
    whole, like those who go down
    to the Pit.
13 We'll find all kinds
    of valuable property
    and fill our houses with plunder.
14 Throw in your lot with us,
    and we'll all share the loot"—
15 my son, don't travel that road
    with them
    or set foot on their path,
16 because their feet run toward evil
    and they hurry to shed blood.
17 It is useless to spread a net
    where any bird can see it,
18 but they set an ambush
    to kill themselves;
    they attack their own lives.
19 Such are the paths of all who make
    profit dishonestly;
    it takes the lives of those
    who receive it.

WISDOM'S PLEA

20 Wisdom calls out in the street;
    she makes her voice heard
    in the public squares.
21 She cries out above the commotion;
    she speaks at the entrance
    of the city gates:
22 "How long, inexperienced ones,
    will you love ignorance?
    How long will you mockers
    enjoy mocking
    and you fools hate knowledge?
23 If you respond to my warning,
    then I will pour out my spirit on you
    and teach you my words.
24 Since I called out and you refused,
    extended my hand and no one
    paid attention,
25 since you neglected all my counsel
    and did not accept my correction,
26 I, in turn, will laugh at your calamity.
    I will mock when terror strikes you,
27 when terror strikes you like a storm
    and your calamity comes
    like a whirlwind,
    when trouble and stress
    overcome you.
28 Then they will call me,
    but I won't answer;
    they will search for me, but won't
    find me.
29 Because they hated knowledge,
    didn't choose to fear the LORD,
30 were not interested in my counsel,
    and rejected all my correction,
31 they will eat the fruit of their way
    and be glutted with
    their own schemes.
32 For the apostasy
    of the inexperienced
    will kill them,
    and the complacency of fools
    will destroy them.
33 But whoever listens to me
    will live securely
    and be undisturbed by the dread
    of danger."

A Journey, Not a Destination

When you consider the need for wisdom in society today, you might automatically think about people who make up the younger generations. And that's certainly true—in fact, Proverbs is written from the perspective of a parent to a child. Solomon wrote much of the book, and in Proverbs 1:4-5 he specifically mentioned the *inexperienced* and *young* as his audience. Whether young in experience, in age, or both, Proverbs promises prudence, knowledge, and discretion.

But Proverbs is not only for the young and inexperienced! In verse 5, Solomon identified a third group of people when he wrote, "let a wise person listen and increase learning." In other words, Proverbs also contains a promise for those who are older in experience, in age, or both. Those who have been walking the journey called Christianity for some time can and should continue to grow in wisdom and then pass that wisdom on to others.

What that means is that wisdom is not a state in which you can fully arrive this side of heaven. No matter what stage of life you're currently in, you need to grow in wisdom. Wisdom is a journey!

Proverbs 1:7 teaches us that wisdom's journey begins with an attitude. Think about it this way—we live in the information age, but the vast amount of information at our fingertips has not made us any wiser than the generations before us. That's because information apart from the fear of God only makes us more informed sinners. The pursuit of wisdom that does not have its starting point in teachability before the Father always ends in dissatisfaction.

Whether young and inexperienced or older with a lifetime of experience, the kind of knowledge we desperately need comes to those who hunger to know God. When we fear God and treasure Christ, we learn true wisdom. Humility before the Lord leads to teachability which produces wisdom!

Since wisdom comes from knowing and delighting in Christ, what are some practical ways you might grow in your affection for Christ?

Why can a person possess a wealth of knowledge and still be a "fool"?

Wisdom's journey begins with an attitude.

MONTH	DAY	YEAR

WISDOM'S WORTH

2 My son, if you accept my words
and store up my commands
   within you,
2 listening closely to wisdom
and directing your heart
   to understanding;
3 furthermore, if you call out
   to insight
and lift your voice to understanding,
4 if you seek it like silver
and search for it
   like hidden treasure,
5 then you will understand the fear
   of the LORD
and discover the knowledge of God.
6 For the LORD gives wisdom;
from his mouth come knowledge
   and understanding.
7 He stores up success for the upright;
He is a shield for those who live
   with integrity
8 so that he may guard the paths
   of justice
and protect the way
   of his faithful followers.
9 Then you will understand
   righteousness, justice,
and integrity—every good path.
10 For wisdom will enter your heart,
and knowledge will delight you.
11 Discretion will watch over you,
and understanding will guard you.

12 It will rescue you from the way
   of evil—
from anyone who says
   perverse things,
13 from those who abandon
   the right paths
to walk in ways of darkness,
14 from those who enjoy doing evil
and celebrate perversion,
15 whose paths are crooked,
and whose ways are devious.
16 It will rescue you
   from a forbidden woman,
from a wayward woman
   with her flattering talk,
17 who abandons the companion
   of her youth
and forgets the covenant of her God;
18 for her house sinks down to death
and her ways to the land
   of the departed spirits.
19 None return who go to her;
none reach the paths of life.
20 So follow the way of the good,
and keep to the paths
   of the righteous.
21 For the upright will inhabit the land,
and those of integrity will remain
   in it;
22 but the wicked will be cut off
   from the land,
and the treacherous ripped out of it.

God's Mouth to Your Ears

What voices are loudest in your life? Do they all agree with you? Who has permission to speak wisdom into your life—both when it feels good and when it hurts a little bit?

In Proverbs 2:6-7, Solomon assures us that true wisdom is only God's to give, and He does give it. But God's wisdom is not always easy to hear. In fact, Jeremiah 23:29 describes God's Word as a fire and a hammer that breaks apart the hardest places. The truth is, sometimes God's wisdom hits us where it hurts. Our natural inclination might be to resist or even reject that wisdom. So we need ears that are ready to receive it and hearts that pursue it. That starts by attentively listening and storing up God's words and commands (Proverbs 2:1).

Being attentive to something means constantly tending to it. This takes consistent and concerted effort. We must regularly lean into God's Word—letting it shape, mold, encourage, inform, and correct us. We must listen for His voice. There is simply no substitute in the life of a believer for time spent with God daily in His Word and prayer.

This is precisely the reason we're seeking to read Proverbs daily. If we are going to walk in God's wisdom each day, we must establish time each day to receive that wisdom. We must surrender to God daily and seek Him so that we will be transformed, and our lives will prove His will.

To move forward in the journey of wisdom, we must tend to the words of God and incline our hearts to understand. Many voices shout for our attention; let's ensure that God's voice is loudest.

What are your ears most attentive to right now? What obstacles keep you from being most attentive to God's Word?

What is a life situation where you need God's Word to shape your understanding?

There is no substitute for time spent with God in His Word and prayer.

TRUST THE LORD

3 My son, don't forget my teaching,
but let your heart keep
my commands;
2 for they will bring you
many days, a full life, and well-being.
3 Never let loyalty and faithfulness
leave you.
Tie them around your neck;
write them on the tablet
of your heart.
4 Then you will find favor
and high regard
with God and people.

5 Trust in the LORD with all your heart,
and do not rely on
your own understanding;
6 in all your ways know him,
and he will make your paths straight.
7 Don't be wise in your own eyes;
fear the LORD and turn away
from evil.
8 This will be healing for your body
and strengthening for your bones.
9 Honor the LORD
with your possessions
and with the first produce
of your entire harvest;
10 then your barns will be
completely filled,
and your vats will overflow
with new wine.
11 Do not despise
the LORD's instruction, my son,
and do not loathe his discipline;
12 for the LORD disciplines the one
he loves,
just as a father disciplines the son in
whom he delights.

WISDOM BRINGS HAPPINESS

13 Happy is a man who finds wisdom
and who acquires understanding,
14 for she is more profitable than silver,
and her revenue is better than gold.
15 She is more precious than jewels;
nothing you desire can equal her.
16 Long life is in her right hand;
in her left, riches and honor.
17 Her ways are pleasant,
and all her paths, peaceful.
18 She is a tree of life to those
who embrace her,
and those who hold on to her
are happy.

19 The LORD founded the earth
by wisdom
and established the heavens
by understanding.
20 By his knowledge the watery depths
broke open,
and the clouds dripped with dew.

21 Maintain sound wisdom
and discretion.
My son, don't lose sight of them.
22 They will be life for you
and adornment for your neck.
23 Then you will go safely on your way;
your foot will not stumble.
24 When you lie down, you will not
be afraid;
you will lie down, and your sleep
will be pleasant.
25 Don't fear sudden danger
or the ruin of the wicked
when it comes,
26 for the LORD will be your confidence
and will keep your foot from a snare.

TREAT OTHERS FAIRLY

27 When it is in your power,
don't withhold good from the one to
whom it belongs.
28 Don't say to your neighbor,
"Go away! Come back later.
I'll give it tomorrow" —
when it is there with you.
29 Don't plan any harm
against your neighbor,
for he trusts you and lives near you.
30 Don't accuse anyone without cause,
when he has done you no harm.
31 Don't envy a violent man
or choose any of his ways;
32 for the devious are detestable
to the LORD,
but he is a friend to the upright.
33 The LORD's curse is on the household
of the wicked,
but he blesses the home
of the righteous;
34 He mocks those who mock
but gives grace to the humble.
35 The wise will inherit honor,
but he holds up fools to dishonor.

When You Don't Know What to Do

If anyone ever had reason to trust in himself, it was Solomon. He was king, he was wise, and there would never be anyone like him ever again (1 Kings 3:5,12). But Solomon understood where his wisdom came from. As much wisdom as Solomon had been given, God's wisdom was far greater. His understanding is beyond measure (Psalm 147:5); the depth of His wisdom is unsearchable (Romans 11:33-36); He knows us better than we know ourselves (1 John 3:20).

Even the wisest among us don't know what to do sometimes, and it's important to acknowledge that. That's why Proverbs 3:5-6 gives us two practices and a promise. The first practice is to trust God (v. 5). We can't trust in the Lord with our whole hearts and also lean on our own understanding. Trusting in the Lord involves a change in posture—from thinking we know what to do to understanding that while we don't know what to do, God always does. God has a plan for our lives broadly, and He also has a plan for every detail of our lives. We are safe and secure when we rely on Him to carry out those plans. We can trust God with everything!

The second practice reveals whether or not we are doing that. When we truly trust God, we know Him in all our ways (v. 6). Other translations use the words *acknowledge* or *follow* here. The point is, wisdom invites God into everything. It is through relationship that God speaks into our lives. You can't compartmentalize that relationship and expect to know what to do when you don't know what to do.

Here's the promise—when you trust God and follow Him in every part of your life, "He will make your paths straight" (v. 6). God will lead you in the direction you need to go and will provide everything along the way.

This means it's okay to not know what to do. We don't need to be consumed with knowing all the answers. Instead, we need to be consumed with knowing God. He will faithfully direct us and accomplish His will through our lives.

In what areas of life do you tend to lean on your own understanding instead of the Lord's?

What would it look like, practically, for you to trust God with all your heart this week?

Trust that God has a plan and follow Him.

MONTH   DAY   YEAR

A FATHER'S EXAMPLE

4 Listen, sons, to a father's discipline,
and pay attention so that
you may gain understanding,
2 for I am giving you good instruction.
Don't abandon my teaching.
3 When I was a son with my father,
tender and precious to my mother,
4 he taught me and said,
"Your heart must hold on
to my words.
Keep my commands and live.
5 Get wisdom, get understanding;
don't forget or turn away
from the words from my mouth.
6 Don't abandon wisdom, and she will
watch over you;
love her, and she will guard you.
7 Wisdom is supreme —
so get wisdom.
And whatever else you get,
get understanding.
8 Cherish her, and she will exalt you;
if you embrace her, she will
honor you.
9 She will place a garland of favor
on your head;
she will give you a crown of beauty."

TWO WAYS OF LIFE

10 Listen, my son. Accept my words,
and you will live many years.
11 I am teaching you the way
of wisdom;
I am guiding you on straight paths.
12 When you walk, your steps will not
be hindered;
when you run, you will not stumble.
13 Hold on to instruction; don't let go.
Guard it, for it is your life.
14 Keep off the path of the wicked;

don't proceed on the way
of evil ones.
15 Avoid it; don't travel on it.
Turn away from it, and pass it by.
16 For they can't sleep
unless they have done what is evil;
they are robbed of sleep
unless they make someone stumble.
17 They eat the bread of wickedness
and drink the wine of violence.
18 The path of the righteous is
like the light of dawn,
shining brighter and brighter
until midday.
19 But the way of the wicked is
like the darkest gloom;
they don't know what makes
them stumble.

THE STRAIGHT PATH

20 My son, pay attention to my words;
listen closely to my sayings.
21 Don't lose sight of them;
keep them within your heart.
22 For they are life to those
who find them,
and health to one's whole body.
23 Guard your heart above all else,
for it is the source of life.
24 Don't let your mouth
speak dishonestly,
and don't let your lips talk deviously.
25 Let your eyes look forward;
fix your gaze straight ahead.
26 Carefully consider the path
for your feet,
and all your ways will be established.
27 Don't turn to the right or to the left;
keep your feet away from evil.

Two Paths, One Choice

God's wisdom is a gift given to us, but we must make the choice to receive it. Using the metaphor of two paths, Proverbs 4 makes that choice plain. Imagine standing at the start of a trail, knowing that one path will lead to certain injury and disappointment, while the other will lead you safely to the most grand and glorious view. That choice would be easy to make, right?

The same principle holds true in our walk with the Lord. There is a "path of the righteous" that shines brightly (v. 18) and a path "of the wicked" that is filled with gloomy darkness (v. 19). The path of the righteous is the journey of wisdom, and the path of the wicked is the journey of foolishness. The path of the righteous is lived inside God's boundaries, and the path of the wicked is lived outside of those boundaries (vv. 20-22,27).

It seems simple—if you carefully consider which path to take, you will choose the wise way (v. 26). Still, there are many deep-thinking people in the world who are on the wrong path. They believe that every path can be a good and right way. They choose a direction that suits their preferences and, in doing so, believe they can find their own truth and walk in it.

The reality, though, is that there is only one truth, and that is what we must carefully consider. The writer of Hebrews put it this way: "Make straight paths for your feet" (Hebrews 12:13). The straight path is the path God gives us in His Word, the one Jesus paved for us, and the one upon which His Spirit leads us. It is the path of healing from whatever stumbling we have previously done and the path of wisdom, certainty, and righteousness for all future steps we take.

Why is it important to evaluate the path you're taking on a regular basis?

What might be some signs you're on the right path? Some signs you're on the wrong path?

There is only one truth, and that is what we must carefully consider.

AVOID SEDUCTION

5 My son, pay attention to my wisdom;
listen closely to my understanding
² so that you may maintain discretion
and your lips safeguard knowledge.
³ Though the lips
of the forbidden woman
drip honey
and her words are smoother than oil,
⁴ in the end she's as bitter
as wormwood
and as sharp as a double-
edged sword.
⁵ Her feet go down to death;
her steps head straight for Sheol.
⁶ She doesn't consider the path of life;
she doesn't know that her ways
are unstable.

⁷ So now, sons, listen to me,
and don't turn away from the words
from my mouth.
⁸ Keep your way far from her.
Don't go near the door of her house.
⁹ Otherwise, you will give up
your vitality to others
and your years to someone cruel;
¹⁰ strangers will drain your resources,
and your hard-earned pay will end
up
in a foreigner's house.
¹¹ At the end of your life,
you will lament
when your physical body
has been consumed,
¹² and you will say,
"How I hated discipline,
and how my heart
despised correction.
¹³ I didn't obey my teachers
or listen closely to my instructors.
¹⁴ I am on the verge of complete ruin
before the entire community."

ENJOY MARRIAGE

¹⁵ Drink water from your own cistern,
water flowing from your own well.
¹⁶ Should your springs flow
in the streets,
streams in the public squares?
¹⁷ They should be for you alone
and not for you to share
with strangers.
¹⁸ Let your fountain be blessed,
and take pleasure in the wife
of your youth.
¹⁹ A loving deer, a graceful doe —
let her breasts always satisfy you;
be lost in her love forever.
²⁰ Why, my son, would you
lose yourself
with a forbidden woman
or embrace a wayward woman?
²¹ For a man's ways are before
the LORD's eyes,
and he considers all his paths.
²² A wicked man's iniquities will
trap him;
he will become tangled in the ropes
of his own sin.
²³ He will die because there is
no discipline,
and be lost because of
his great stupidity.

The Way to Avoid Danger

If we had started this study by listing the top ten areas of life where wisdom is needed in our culture, sex would likely be somewhere near the top. We live in a sex-saturated culture, but our culture's view on sex tends to be contrary to that of Scripture.

Our culture proudly emphasizes everything about sex except for God's plan. And, truth be told, the message given to us might seem good and right (v. 3), but what seems good and right in the world leads us away from God's wisdom, not toward it (v. 4). God has given us the wisdom we need. In fact, Scripture has a lot to say about God's design for sexual intimacy.

After warning his son of the dangers of seduction and adultery, Solomon gave him wisdom about how to avoid those dangers—find pleasure in your wife (v. 18) and "be lost in her love forever" (v. 19). God wants both wives and husbands to enjoy each other, and when the Bible speaks romantically, it always assumes monogamy and marriage. This is true romance: to love and enjoy your husband or wife all the days of your life.

Solomon loved his wife, and it was evident in his words and actions. However, 1 Kings 11 tells us that Solomon didn't avoid danger. This wise man very foolishly took many women as his wives and that sin turned his heart away from the Lord.

There were consequences. God didn't tell Solomon how to live, and then step back and become an observer. Solomon's foolish actions grieved God, and He tore the kingdom out of Solomon's hands. It is impossible to hide any sin from the Lord. He is all-seeing and all-knowing, and He wants better for us than a life bound by the seduction of the world.

What is a danger you need the wisdom of God's Word to help you avoid?

If you are married, what can you do to express your delight in your spouse and God? If you are not married, what can you do to express your delight in God and in any potential spouse you may have in the future?

The world leads us away from God's wisdom, not toward it.

FINANCIAL ENTANGLEMENTS

6 ¹ My son, if you have put up security
for your neighbor
or entered into an agreement
with a stranger,
² you have been snared by the words
of your mouth—
trapped by the words
from your mouth.
³ Do this, then, my son,
and free yourself,
for you have put yourself
in your neighbor's power:
Go, humble yourself, and plead
with your neighbor.
⁴ Don't give sleep to your eyes
or slumber to your eyelids.
⁵ Escape like a gazelle from a hunter,
like a bird from a hunter's trap.

LAZINESS

⁶ Go to the ant, you slacker!
Observe its ways and become wise.
⁷ Without leader, administrator,
or ruler,
⁸ it prepares its provisions in summer;
it gathers its food during harvest.
⁹ How long will you stay in bed,
you slacker?
When will you get up
from your sleep?
¹⁰ A little sleep, a little slumber,
a little folding of the arms to rest,
¹¹ and your poverty will come like
a robber,
your need, like a bandit.

THE MALICIOUS MAN

¹² A worthless person, a wicked man
goes around speaking dishonestly,
¹³ winking his eyes, signaling
with his feet,
and gesturing with his fingers.
¹⁴ He always plots evil with perversity
in his heart;
he stirs up trouble.
¹⁵ Therefore calamity
will strike him suddenly;
he will be shattered instantly,
beyond recovery.

WHAT THE LORD HATES

¹⁶ The LORD hates six things;
in fact, seven are detestable to him:
¹⁷ arrogant eyes, a lying tongue,
hands that shed innocent blood,
¹⁸ a heart that plots wicked schemes,
feet eager to run to evil,
¹⁹ a lying witness who gives
false testimony,
and one who stirs up trouble
among brothers.

WARNING AGAINST ADULTERY

²⁰ My son, keep
your father's command,
and don't reject
your mother's teaching.
²¹ Always bind them to your heart;
tie them around your neck.
²² When you walk here and there,
they will guide you;
when you lie down, they will
watch over you;
when you wake up, they will
talk to you.
²³ For a command is a lamp,
teaching is a light,
and corrective discipline is the way
to life.
²⁴ They will protect you
from an evil woman,
from the flattering tongue of
a wayward woman.
²⁵ Don't lust in your heart
for her beauty
or let her captivate you
with her eyelashes.
²⁶ For a prostitute's fee is only a loaf
of bread,
but the wife of another man goes
after a precious life.
²⁷ Can a man embrace fire
and his clothes not be burned?
²⁸ Can a man walk on burning coals
without scorching his feet?
²⁹ So it is with the one who sleeps with
another man's wife;
no one who touches her
will go unpunished.
³⁰ People don't despise the thief
if he steals
to satisfy himself when he is hungry.
³¹ Still, if caught, he must pay
seven times as much;
he must give up all the wealth
in his house.
³² The one who commits adultery
lacks sense;
whoever does so destroys himself.
³³ He will get a beating and dishonor,
and his disgrace will
never be removed.
³⁴ For jealousy enrages a husband,
and he will show no mercy
when he takes revenge.
³⁵ He will not be appeased by anything
or be persuaded by lavish bribes.

Light for Your Life

Think about a time you've experienced a power outage. When everything goes dark, especially at night, you want to find a source of light, right? Without light, we can't see where we're going. Proverbs 6:23 tells us the same principle holds true in our spiritual lives—without the light of God's Word, we all stumble through life. We don't know where to go or what to do. But God gave us His Word to show us His way in the midst of the darkness of this world.

Proverbs 6 calls attention to some specific areas where we might stumble in the dark—issues of finance (vv. 1-5), work ethic (vv. 6-11), dealing with dishonest and arrogant people who stir up trouble (vv. 12-19), and sexual temptation (vv. 20-35). We live in these realities; still, many of us don't seek God daily in His Word. Instead, we walk in the dark with fear, anxiety, frustration, stress, and confusion, wondering why we don't know what to do.

God has given us the light of His Word to direct our steps in every dark place we might find ourselves. He doesn't want to steal our joy. Neither does He want us to continue in confusion, anxiety, and frustration. God's wisdom in His Word leads us to get the most out of this life for which He created us. He wants us to enjoy life!

God doesn't only want us to enjoy life on vacation; He shows us how to enjoy life in our daily work. He doesn't only show us how to enjoy life in the very best years of marriage; He shows us how to enjoy life when we're single or when marriage brings challenges. We face temptations all through life—how to spend our money or our time, and how to think, speak, and act in many other contexts. Those who pursue wisdom will turn to the light of God's Word and trust that He knows best, always binding His commands to their hearts (v. 21). What does God promise to those who do that? He will give us the direction, protection, and counsel we need (v. 22).

What is a past situation in which you were guided by God's Word?

In what current situation do you need to turn to the light of God's Word for direction?

We cannot know God's will apart from God's Word.

7

My son, obey my words,
and treasure my commands.
2 Keep my commands and live,
and guard my instructions
as you would the pupil of your eye.
3 Tie them to your fingers;
write them on the tablet
of your heart.
4 Say to wisdom, "You are my sister,"
and call understanding your relative.
5 She will keep you
from a forbidden woman,
a wayward woman with
her flattering talk.

A STORY OF SEDUCTION

6 At the window of my house
I looked through my lattice.
7 I saw among the inexperienced,
I noticed among the youths,
a young man lacking sense.
8 Crossing the street near her corner,
he strolled down the road
to her house
9 at twilight, in the evening,
in the dark of the night.
10 A woman came to meet him
dressed like a prostitute,
having a hidden agenda.
11 She is loud and defiant;
her feet do not stay at home.
12 Now in the street,
now in the squares,
she lurks at every corner.
13 She grabs him and kisses him;
she brazenly says to him,
14 "I've made fellowship offerings;
today I've fulfilled my vows.

15 So I came out to meet you,
to search for you, and I've found you.
16 I've spread coverings on my bed—
richly colored linen from Egypt.
17 I've perfumed my bed
with myrrh, aloes, and cinnamon.
18 Come, let's drink deeply
of lovemaking until morning.
Let's feast on each other's love!
19 My husband isn't home;
he went on a long journey.
20 He took a bag of silver with him
and will come home at the time
of the full moon."
21 She seduces him
with her persistent pleading;
she lures with her flattering talk.
22 He follows her impulsively
like an ox going to the slaughter,
like a deer bounding toward a trap
23 until an arrow pierces its liver,
like a bird darting into a snare—
he doesn't know it will cost him
his life.

24 Now, sons, listen to me,
and pay attention to the words
from my mouth.
25 Don't let your heart turn aside
to her ways;
don't stray onto her paths.
26 For she has brought many
down to death;
her victims are countless.
27 Her house is the road to Sheol,
descending to the chambers
of death.

Wisdom Exceeds Intention

Saying the right thing in a given situation is fairly easy. Yet, it is something else entirely to act in accordance with the things we say. Anyone can make a statement that sounds good and is approved by others, but we show the worth of our words when we back up our words with action that shows we truly mean what we say.

Another way to say this is that wisdom isn't found in mere intellectual assent or even the very best of intentions; wisdom requires action. We may intend to follow Christ faithfully in the wisdom He gives, but unless we follow this intention with action and direction—our intention does us no good.

Many people resist God's wisdom entirely because of the gulf between wisdom and action. They struggle to reconcile the hypocrisy of words and actions that do not match.

But the father in Proverbs 7 didn't want the wisdom he gave his son to simply be "a good idea my dad shared one time." God's wisdom is far more than that. So the father implored his son to let the wisdom he received exceed intention. Regarding those wise instructions, the father used words like *obey*, *treasure*, *keep*, and *guard* (vv. 1-2). He told him to tie them to his fingers, and write them on the tablet of his heart (v. 3). Then to drive the point home even further, he told him a story of seduction (vv. 6-27).

The father had seen with his own eyes the failure of good intentions when a young man gave into seduction. Because the young man did not obey, treasure, keep, and guard God's wisdom, he paid the full price—his life. The father knew his own son, like all of us, would be deceived by and attracted to forbidden things in life. He couldn't emphasize wisdom for him—or us—enough. God's instructions are not merely good knowledge or intentions to possess; they are a life-giving treasure we must choose to live out daily.

Why is all of the Christian life a call toward good action and not only good intention?

Why is it so difficult for people to receive God's wisdom related to the subject of sex?

Wisdom requires action.

WEEK 2

Receiving Wisdom from the Word

PROVERBS 8-14

Wisdom's Humility

In your first week of study, you may have found yourself alternately thinking about yourself and others you know—some wise and some unwise. None of us demonstrate wisdom all the time, but all of us want wisdom. We want to receive wisdom and we want to be able to offer wisdom to others. The problem is, pride often gets in the way.

In this second week of study, God will continue to give us His everlasting wisdom for everyday life. But receiving it and extending it to other people requires us to humble ourselves (Proverbs 11:2). To receive wisdom, we have to put ourselves in a position to learn. We have to submit, listen, and acknowledge our own insufficiency. We must place ourselves under God's wisdom and alongside others He is also making wise, recognizing the answers we don't have on our own.

To be able to offer wisdom to someone else we must remain humble. The wise person doesn't share "wisdom" so others consider him or her wise. In fact, the wise person humbly recognizes his or her own moments and seasons of foolishness and doesn't pretend to know all the answers. The wise person simply aims to show others what he or she has learned along the way.

Humility and teachability are rare in this world. People generally think they have the answers they need. But the gospel calls us to a different way. Just as we were insufficient to attain our own salvation, we are insufficient to attain wisdom by our own understanding. As we continue our study in Proverbs this week, let's each humbly agree, "I don't know everything. But I want to learn."

Start

Use this page to introduce the idea and then get the conversation started.

Share something that stood out to you in last week's study of Proverbs 1–7.

The primary way that God gives wisdom is through His Word. If we value God's wisdom, we will value His Word. Likewise, if we neglect His Word, we neglect His wisdom. Consider your tendencies when it comes to seeking God's wisdom in your life.

When you're unsure how to do something, are you more likely to: read the instructions, watch an online video, ask someone for help, or just forge ahead assuming you'll figure it out along the way? Why?

What about in your spiritual life? When you're unsure what to do, are you more likely to: personally search God's Word, search the internet for a sermon or blog on that topic, ask someone you know for advice, or just forge ahead assuming you'll figure it out along the way? Why?

Pray

Thank God for the wisdom found in His Word.
Ask Him to show you how to receive it.

Watch

Use this page to take notes as you watch the group teaching session.

To access the teaching sessions, use the instructions in the back of your Bible study book.

Discuss

Use this section to discuss the video teaching.

The phrase, "The word of the Lord came to" appears about one hundred times throughout the pages of Scripture. God spoke to His people then and He speaks to us now. How has God spoken to you? Do you expect God to speak to you? Why?

Read Isaiah 55:10-11. What is God's intention in giving us His Word? What is God's Word accomplishing in the world? How has God's Word succeeded in your life?

What are some situations where we might wish God would show us the way? Read Proverbs 6:23a. Why is it impossible to see the way apart from the Word of God?

"Corrective discipline is the way to life" (6:23b). Vance explained, "God, in His Word, corrects those things that are wrong so that He can position us to enjoy life to the fullest." Why is this hard for many people to believe? Why is it important that we do believe it?

Vance said, "A wise way to live is to give priority to hearing from God daily through His Word." Practically, what does that involve? Is it simply reading Scripture, or is there something else required to hear from God daily?

Read Proverbs 6:20-21. In your own words, what does it mean for your heart to be bound to God's wisdom? Is that kind of attitude of treasuring God's wisdom the automatic daily posture for every believer or is it a process? Explain.

Read James 1:22-25. Based on these verses, what does it mean to truly receive wisdom from the Word? How does this speak to the process of learning to treasure God's wisdom?

Read Proverbs 6:22. What promises does God make about His Word? How do these promises relate to daily life?

MONTH   DAY   YEAR

WISDOM'S APPEAL

8 Doesn't wisdom call out?
Doesn't understanding make
    her voice heard?

2 At the heights overlooking the road,
at the crossroads, she takes
    her stand.

3 Beside the gates leading into the city,
at the main entrance, she cries out:

4 "People, I call out to you;
my cry is to the children of Adam.

5 Learn to be shrewd,
    you who are inexperienced;
develop common sense,
    you who are foolish.

6 Listen, for I speak of noble things,
and what my lips say is right.

7 For my mouth tells the truth,
and wickedness is detestable
    to my lips.

8 All the words from my mouth
    are righteous;
none of them are deceptive
    or perverse.

9 All of them are clear
    to the perceptive,
and right to those
    who discover knowledge.

10 Accept my instruction
    instead of silver,
and knowledge rather
    than pure gold.

11 For wisdom is better than jewels,
and nothing desirable can equal it.

12 I, wisdom, share a home
    with shrewdness
and have knowledge and discretion.

13 To fear the Lord is to hate evil.
I hate arrogant pride, evil conduct,
and perverse speech.

14 I possess good advice
    and sound wisdom;
I have understanding and strength.

15 It is by me that kings reign
and rulers enact just law;

16 by me, princes lead,
as do nobles and all righteous judges.

17 I love those who love me,
and those who search for me
    find me.

18 With me are riches and honor,
lasting wealth and righteousness.

19 My fruit is better than solid gold,
and my harvest than pure silver.

20 I walk in the ways of righteousness,
along the paths of justice,

21 giving wealth as an inheritance
    to those who love me,
and filling their treasuries.

22 "The Lord acquired me
at the beginning of his creation,
before his works of long ago.

23 I was formed before ancient times,
from the beginning,
    before the earth began.

24 I was born
when there were no watery depths
and no springs filled with water.

25 Before the mountains
    were established,
prior to the hills, I was given birth —

26 before he made the land, the fields,
or the first soil on earth.

27 I was there when he established
    the heavens,
when he laid out the horizon
    on the surface
    of the ocean,

28 when he placed the skies above,
when the fountains of the ocean
    gushed out,

29 when he set a limit for the sea
so that the waters would not violate
    his command,
when he laid out the foundations
    of the earth.

30 I was a skilled craftsman beside him.
I was his delight every day,
always rejoicing before him.

31 I was rejoicing in
    his inhabited world,
delighting in the children of Adam.

32 "And now, sons, listen to me;
those who keep my ways are happy.

33 Listen to instruction and be wise;
don't ignore it.

34 Anyone who listens to me is happy,
watching at my doors every day,
waiting by the posts of my doorway.

35 For the one who finds me finds life
and obtains favor from the Lord,

36 but the one who misses me
    harms himself;
all who hate me love death."

The Choice is Yours

In Proverbs 8, wisdom is personified to help us see that God's everlasting wisdom for everyday life is for everyone. The question posed in verse 1, "Doesn't wisdom call out?" is answered in verses 2-36 with a resounding yes! She doesn't call out in a secret room of a secret club where only those who have a secret password can enter. Rather, she cries out impartially in the most well-traveled spaces (vv. 2-3).

In our human nature, we lack wisdom. We need wisdom. And, as much as we may struggle to find it, wisdom isn't hiding from us. God hasn't secluded the good and right way to think and live so that only a few special people find it. The truth is, if we remain unwise it is because we have chosen not to listen to God's instruction and follow it.

Wisdom, then, is a choice we make each and every day about whether or not we will hear and listen to God's Word. Proverbs 8 assures us that the wisdom of God's Word is true, righteous, clear, valuable, sound, strong, and a well-established foundation that illuminates our way. Those who search for this wisdom will certainly find it (v. 17)!

God wants all of us to listen to His instruction because He loves us and wants us to enjoy the life we've been given. He calls out to us to receive and embrace His wisdom, so that we might experience the very best possible life here on earth and throughout eternity. But we have a choice. God will not force His design for our lives on us. He will continue to invite us into that perfect design and give us a choice whether to receive it or not.

Practically speaking, how has God's wisdom called out to you in the past? How is God's wisdom calling out to you now?

Read verses 35-36 again. Describe the contrast given. How does choosing to not listen to God's wisdom harm you?

Wisdom isn't hiding from us.

WISDOM VERSUS FOOLISHNESS

9 Wisdom has built her house;
she has carved out her seven pillars.
2 She has prepared her meat;
she has mixed her wine;
she has also set her table.
3 She has sent out her female servants;
she calls out from the highest points
of the city:
4 "Whoever is inexperienced,
enter here!"
To the one who lacks sense, she says,
5 "Come, eat my bread,
and drink the wine I have mixed.
6 Leave inexperience behind,
and you will live;
pursue the way of understanding.
7 The one who corrects a mocker
will bring abuse on himself;
the one who rebukes the wicked
will get hurt.
8 Don't rebuke a mocker, or he will
hate you;
rebuke the wise, and he will
love you.
9 Instruct the wise, and he will be
wiser still;
teach the righteous, and he will
learn more.

10 "The fear of the Lord is
the beginning of wisdom,
and the knowledge of the Holy One
is understanding.
11 For by me your days will be many,
and years will be added to your life.
12 If you are wise, you are wise
for your own benefit;
if you mock, you alone will bear
the consequences."

13 Folly is a rowdy woman;
she is gullible and knows nothing.
14 She sits by the doorway
of her house,
on a seat at the highest point
of the city,
15 calling to those who pass by,
who go straight ahead on their paths:
16 "Whoever is inexperienced,
enter here!"
To the one who lacks sense, she says,
17 "Stolen water is sweet,
and bread eaten secretly is tasty!"
18 But he doesn't know
that the departed spirits are there,
that her guests are in the depths
of Sheol.

Folly's Worldview is Shortsighted

We have seen that everlasting wisdom for everyday life calls out to us and receiving it is a choice we must make in response. Proverbs 9 continues this theme, and adds a stark reminder—there is more than one voice vying for our attention. As wisdom calls out to us, so does foolishness.

This has been depicted often in animation and comics as characters wrestle with the choice between wisdom and folly. An angelic figure appears on one shoulder, a devilish figure on the other, and advice is given by both. They make their cases until the character makes his or her choice—wisdom or folly.

While this plot device is often used humorously, the reality of the competing calls of wisdom and folly serve as a warning for us. Wisdom and folly are vastly different in both intention and outcome.

Unlike wisdom, who invites us to leave behind naivete and pursue the knowledge of God, folly invites us to only embrace the simplicity of human desire. And that invitation is not given in a way that we might miss it. Folly is boisterous, calling us loudly. She offers no wisdom; rather, she favors ignorance, which better suits her purpose and worldview—take whatever is desired and be accountable to no one (v. 17).

The problem is that folly's purpose and worldview is incredibly shortsighted. None of us live life apart from accountability. Verse 18 makes that clear. When you live outside of God's boundaries—outside of His wisdom—it ends in disaster. A life lived in the foolishness of sin costs you everything.

What phrase about wisdom in Proverbs 9 stands out as particularly helpful or instructive? What phrase about folly stands out? Why?

God calls out wisdom to offer life. Satan calls out foolishness to offer death. What steps can you take to be less vulnerable to Satan's temptations?

Living outside of God's boundaries ends in disaster.

MONTH	DAY	YEAR

A COLLECTION OF SOLOMON'S PROVERBS

10 Solomon's proverbs:

A wise son brings joy to his father,
but a foolish son, heartache to his mother.

2 Ill-gotten gains do not profit anyone,
but righteousness rescues from death.

3 The LORD will not let the righteous
go hungry,
but he denies the wicked what they crave.

4 Idle hands make one poor,
but diligent hands bring riches.

5 The son who gathers during summer
is prudent;
the son who sleeps during harvest
is disgraceful.

6 Blessings are on the head of the righteous,
but the mouth of the wicked
conceals violence.

7 The remembrance of the righteous is
a blessing,
but the name of the wicked will rot.

8 A wise heart accepts commands,
but foolish lips will be destroyed.

9 The one who lives with integrity
lives securely,
but whoever perverts his ways will be
found out.

10 A sly wink of the eye causes grief,
and foolish lips will be destroyed.

11 The mouth of the righteous is a fountain
of life,
but the mouth of the wicked
conceals violence.

12 Hatred stirs up conflicts,
but love covers all offenses.

13 Wisdom is found on the lips
of the discerning,
but a rod is for the back of the one
who lacks sense.

14 The wise store up knowledge,
but the mouth of the fool
hastens destruction.

15 The wealth of the rich is his fortified city;
the poverty of the poor is
their destruction.

16 The reward of the righteous is life;
the wages of the wicked is punishment.

17 The one who follows instruction is
on the path to life,
but the one who rejects correction
goes astray.

18 The one who conceals hatred has
lying lips,
and whoever spreads slander is a fool.

19 When there are many words,
sin is unavoidable,
but the one who controls his lips
is prudent.

20 The tongue of the righteous is pure silver;
the heart of the wicked is of little value.

21 The lips of the righteous feed many,
but fools die for lack of sense.

22 The LORD's blessing enriches,
and he adds no painful effort to it.

23 As shameful conduct is pleasure for a fool,
so wisdom is for a person
of understanding.

24 What the wicked dreads will come to him,
but what the righteous desire will be given
to them.

25 When the whirlwind passes,
the wicked are no more,
but the righteous are secure forever.

26 Like vinegar to the teeth and smoke
to the eyes,
so the slacker is to the one who sends him
on an errand.

27 The fear of the LORD prolongs life,
but the years of the wicked are cut short.

28 The hope of the righteous is joy,
but the expectation of the wicked
will perish.

29 The way of the LORD is a stronghold
for the honorable,
but destruction awaits evildoers.

30 The righteous will never be shaken,
but the wicked will not remain
on the earth.

31 The mouth of the righteous
produces wisdom,
but a perverse tongue will be cut out.

32 The lips of the righteous know
what is appropriate,
but the mouth of the wicked,
only what is perverse.

Talk Less, Listen More

Proverbs 10 covers a lot of topical ground, but if you look closely, you'll find repetition of one particular theme. In fact, go ahead and mark every verse you find that mentions the mouth, lips, or tongue.

Again and again in Proverbs 10 we're reminded of the foolishness and wisdom we demonstrate with words. We tend to minimize the consequence of our speech, reasoning, "They're just words." But Scripture assures us that our words matter greatly, and Jesus told us "the mouth speaks from the overflow of the heart" (Luke 6:45). So they're not "just" words. They're a reflection of our hearts. And what our words often show is that our hearts need to change.

That change of heart we all need begins with a decision to listen. Think of it this way: your mouth is connected to your heart, and your heart is connected to your ears! Proverbs 10:14 puts it this way, "The wise store up knowledge." How do you store up knowledge? It's certainly not by talking (v. 19)! No, you store up knowledge by listening. Wisdom listens.

Verse 17 carries the principle even further, teaching that those who listen and follow instruction are "on the path to life," but those who do not listen and reject correction "go astray." You see, wisdom doesn't only listen to instruction that agrees with its point of view; it listens even when instruction confronts that point of view and calls for certain change.

We are tempted to quickly explain, defend, excuse, or justify our thoughts, attitudes, or behaviors. Instead, we need to be willing to humbly listen to godly correction and instruction—the type of listening that goes beyond merely hearing, in one ear and out the other, but results in an active and obedient faith.

What are some practical ways God instructs and corrects us? How does He speak to us?

What point of correction has God's wisdom confronted you with in this study so far? What choices do you have in responding to that correction?

Wisdom listens to correction.

11 Dishonest scales are detestable
to the LORD,
but an accurate weight is his delight.

2 When arrogance comes, disgrace follows,
but with humility comes wisdom.

3 The integrity of the upright guides them,
but the perversity of the treacherous
destroys them.

4 Wealth is not profitable on a day of wrath,
but righteousness rescues from death.

5 The righteousness of the blameless
clears his path,
but the wicked person will fall because of
his wickedness.

6 The righteousness of the upright
rescues them,
but the treacherous are trapped
by their own desires.

7 When the wicked person dies,
his expectation comes to nothing,
and hope placed in wealth vanishes.

8 The righteous one is rescued from trouble;
in his place, the wicked one goes in.

9 With his mouth the ungodly
destroys his neighbor,
but through knowledge the righteous
are rescued.

10 When the righteous thrive, a city rejoices;
when the wicked die, there is
joyful shouting.

11 A city is built up by the blessing
of the upright,
but it is torn down by the mouth
of the wicked.

12 Whoever shows contempt
for his neighbor lacks sense,
but a person with understanding
keeps silent.

13 A gossip goes around revealing a secret,
but a trustworthy person keeps
a confidence.

14 Without guidance, a people will fall,
but with many counselors
there is deliverance.

15 If someone puts up security for a stranger,
he will suffer for it,
but the one who hates such agreements
is protected.

16 A gracious woman gains honor,
but violent people gain only riches.

17 A kind man benefits himself,
but a cruel person brings ruin on himself.

18 The wicked person earns an empty wage,
but the one who sows righteousness,
a true reward.

19 Genuine righteousness leads to life,
but pursuing evil leads to death.

20 Those with twisted minds are detestable
to the LORD,
but those with blameless conduct are
his delight.

21 Be assured that a wicked person
will not go unpunished,
but the offspring of the righteous
will escape.

22 A beautiful woman who rejects
good sense
is like a gold ring in a pig's snout.

23 The desire of the righteous turns out well,
but the hope of the wicked leads to wrath.

24 One person gives freely,
yet gains more;
another withholds what is right,
only to become poor.

25 A generous person will be enriched,
and the one who gives a drink of water
will receive water.

26 People will curse anyone
who hoards grain,
but a blessing will come to the one
who sells it.

27 The one who searches for what is good
seeks favor,
but if someone looks for trouble,
it will come to him.

28 Anyone trusting in his riches will fall,
but the righteous will flourish like foliage.

29 The one who brings ruin on his household
will inherit the wind,
and a fool will be a slave
to someone whose heart is wise.

30 The fruit of the righteous is a tree of life,
but a cunning person takes lives.

31 If the righteous will be repaid on earth,
how much more the wicked and sinful.

Righteous Promises

Some people believe that hard-nosed, intimidating ruthlessness is the only path to success. They value wealth at all costs, even viewing that single-minded pursuit as the way of wisdom. At times, this attitude does seem to help people get ahead in life. But we should not be fooled. Their success begins and ends with the material.

Proverbs 11 teaches another way, where success comes here on earth and continues on throughout eternity. That way values righteousness more than riches and lives by God's standard and design.

We should understand that living by God's standard and design isn't easy or popular in today's culture. Life is filled with difficult decisions that tempt us to devalue the priority of righteous living—to exchange God's wisdom for worldly "wisdom." However, we must remember that whatever difficulty we face in life is only temporary. God delights in those who seek Him and promises to rescue and deliver those who turn to Him and walk in His righteousness. This is not only a promise for the life to come, but also for our days here on earth.

Pursuing righteousness, then, is not only something we do because we should; we pursue righteousness because it is good for our souls, both now and for eternity. Righteousness rescues us from sin and death (vv. 4,6,8,9,21). It brings us joy and reward (vv. 10,18). It clears our path (v. 5), causes us to flourish (v. 28), and repays us with life-giving fruit (vv. 30,31). Righteousness turns out well and leads to eternal life (vv. 19,23).

What changes would take place in your life this week if you were to truly value righteousness over riches?

What are the promises for those who walk in righteousness? For those who walk in unrighteousness?

Wisdom values righteousness over riches.

12

Whoever loves discipline
loves knowledge,
but one who hates correction is stupid.

2   One who is good obtains favor
from the LORD,
but he condemns a person who schemes.

3   No one can be made secure
by wickedness,
but the root of the righteous
is immovable.

4   A wife of noble character is
her husband's crown,
but a wife who causes shame
is like rottenness in his bones.

5   The thoughts of the righteous are just,
but guidance from the wicked is deceitful.

6   The words of the wicked are
a deadly ambush,
but the speech of the upright
rescues them.

7   The wicked are overthrown and perish,
but the house of the righteous will stand.

8   A man is praised for his insight,
but a twisted mind is despised.

9   Better to be disregarded, yet have
a servant,
than to act important but have no food.

10   The righteous cares about
his animal's health,
but even the merciful acts of the wicked
are cruel.

11   The one who works his land will have
plenty of food,
but whoever chases fantasies lacks sense.

12   The wicked desire what evil people
have caught,
but the root of the righteous is productive.

13   By rebellious speech an evil person
is trapped,
but a righteous person escapes
from trouble.

14   A person will be satisfied with good
by the fruit of his mouth,
and the work of a person's hands
will reward him.

15   A fool's way is right in his own eyes,
but whoever listens to counsel is wise.

16   A fool's displeasure is known at once,
but whoever ignores an insult is sensible.

17   Whoever speaks the truth declares
what is right,
but a false witness speaks deceit.

18   There is one who speaks rashly,
like a piercing sword;
but the tongue of the wise brings healing.

19   Truthful lips endure forever,
but a lying tongue, only a moment.

20   Deceit is in the hearts of those
who plot evil,
but those who promote peace have joy.

21   No disaster overcomes the righteous,
but the wicked are full of misery.

22   Lying lips are detestable to the LORD,
but faithful people are his delight.

23   A shrewd person conceals knowledge,
but a foolish heart publicizes stupidity.

24   The diligent hand will rule,
but laziness will lead to forced labor.

25   Anxiety in a person's heart
weighs it down,
but a good word cheers it up.

26   A righteous person is careful in dealing
with his neighbor,
but the ways of the wicked
lead them astray.

27   A lazy hunter doesn't roast his game,
but to a diligent person, his wealth
is precious.

28   There is life in the path of righteousness,
and in its path there is no death.

More Input Needed

We often think in terms of opposites—right or wrong, light or dark, truth or lie. It is easy to see other people in these clear categories. At the same time, many of us have a hard time believing that our own words and decisions can be defined by such lines. As we examine our own lives, we tend to think in shades of gray.

Proverbs, though, functions on the principle of opposites, reminding us that God calls us to the highest standard, and His standard does not allow any wiggle room. In the first four verses of chapter 12 alone, we see the choice between love and hate, favor and condemnation, security and insecurity, noble character and shame. The contrasts continue in each verse, assuring us we can't have it both ways. For instance, verse 22 teaches us that the Lord detests lying lips, and sees lying as an antonym of faithfulness. As much as we might attempt to reason otherwise, lying and faithfulness cannot coexist as compatible traits in a person's relationship with the Lord.

We want to walk in wisdom. However, left to ourselves, we don't always see our choices clearly defined as either foolish or wise. Because we tend to view our own lives in shades of gray, we need help. We cannot trust our own reasoning. Left unchecked, we think our way is right (v. 15). This is why God's Word exhorts us to seek wise counsel. Wisdom always seeks input when making decisions.

Identify one contrast made in Proverbs 12 that you have, at some point in life, struggled to see as clear opposites. Who, if anyone, helped you understand God's standard regarding that issue?

What is your responsibility in living out the implications of verse 15? What is the responsibility of other believers in helping you live that out?

Seek wise counsel.

13 A wise son responds to his
father's discipline,
but a mocker doesn't listen
to rebuke.

2 From the fruit of his mouth,
a person will enjoy good things,
but treacherous people have
an appetite for violence.

3 The one who guards his mouth
protects his life;
the one who opens his lips invites
his own ruin.

4 The slacker craves, yet has nothing,
but the diligent is fully satisfied.

5 The righteous hate lying,
but the wicked bring
disgust and shame.

6 Righteousness guards people
of integrity,
but wickedness undermines
the sinner.

7 One person pretends to be rich
but has nothing;
another pretends to be poor but has
abundant wealth.

8 Riches are a ransom
for a person's life,
but a poor person hears no threat.

9 The light of the righteous
shines brightly,
but the lamp of the wicked
is put out.

10 Arrogance leads to nothing
but strife,
but wisdom is gained by those
who take advice.

11 Wealth obtained by fraud
will dwindle,
but whoever earns it through labor
will multiply it.

12 Hope delayed makes the heart sick,
but desire fulfilled is a tree of life.

13 The one who has contempt
for instruction
will pay the penalty,
but the one who respects
a command will be rewarded.

14 A wise person's instruction is
a fountain of life,
turning people away from the snares
of death.

15 Good sense wins favor,
but the way of the treacherous
never changes.

16 Every sensible person
acts knowledgeably,
but a fool displays his stupidity.

17 A wicked envoy falls into trouble,
but a trustworthy courier
brings healing.

18 Poverty and disgrace come to those
who ignore discipline,
but the one who accepts correction
will be honored.

19 Desire fulfilled is sweet to the taste,
but to turn from evil is detestable
to fools.

20 The one who walks with the wise
will become wise,
but a companion of fools
will suffer harm.

21 Disaster pursues sinners,
but good rewards the righteous.

22 A good man leaves an inheritance
to his grandchildren,
but the sinner's wealth is stored up
for the righteous.

23 The uncultivated field of the poor
yields abundant food,
but without justice, it is swept away.

24 The one who will not use the rod
hates his son,
but the one who loves him
disciplines him diligently.

25 A righteous person eats
until he is satisfied,
but the stomach of the wicked
is empty.

It's All About Relationships

Every day, we feel the tug of culture pulling us away from the things of God. We are living in a culture that says: the external matters more than the internal, what is popular matters more than what is right, my way matters more than God's way, the temporal matters more than the eternal, and my definition of truth matters more than any other definition of truth.

How, then, can we possibly make wise decisions, maintain a right perspective, and guard our lives from being subverted or twisted by wickedness? What can keep us from a life of compromise?

According to Proverbs 13:6, the answer is to walk in integrity. Sin will constantly try to pull us away and tear us down. But by integrity, we can walk securely in the truth and peace of God. Integrity is a big deal! Integrity means our public lives line up with our private lives. It means what we say lines up with what we do. It is a lifestyle that honors God. And integrity begins on the inside.

As much as we may try to follow a list of rules to change outward behaviors, that pursuit will leave us empty and unchanged on the inside. But by focusing on intimacy with God, His life in us will overflow to change our outward behaviors.

We must pursue intimacy with the Lord so He will transform us from the inside out and make us people of integrity. And, as we do that, Proverbs 13:20 teaches us that we are wise to choose to walk alongside other people who are engaged in that same holy process. Everlasting wisdom for everyday life is all about relationships—the relationship we have with the Lord, and the relationships we have with other believers. We grow in wisdom as we walk together in wisdom.

What dangers are people of integrity guarded from?

How have you personally experienced the truth of verse 20?

Walk in integrity. Walk alongside people of integrity.

14 Every wise woman builds her house,
but a foolish one tears it down
with her own hands.

2 Whoever lives with integrity
fears the LORD,
but the one who is devious in his ways
despises him.

3 The proud speech of a fool brings a rod
of discipline,
but the lips of the wise protect them.

4 Where there are no oxen, the
feeding trough is empty,
but an abundant harvest comes through
the strength of an ox.

5 An honest witness does not deceive,
but a dishonest witness utters lies.

6 A mocker seeks wisdom
and doesn't find it,
but knowledge comes easily
to the perceptive.

7 Stay away from a foolish person;
you will gain no knowledge
from his speech.

8 The sensible person's wisdom is
to consider his way,
but the stupidity of fools deceives them.

9 Fools mock at making reparation,
but there is goodwill among the upright.

10 The heart knows its own bitterness,
and no outsider shares in its joy.

11 The house of the wicked will be destroyed,
but the tent of the upright will flourish.

12 There is a way that seems right
to a person,
but its end is the way to death.

13 Even in laughter a heart may be sad,
and joy may end in grief.

14 The disloyal one will get
what his conduct deserves,
and a good one, what his deeds deserve.

15 The inexperienced one believes anything,
but the sensible one watches his steps.

16 A wise person is cautious and turns
from evil,
but a fool is easily angered and is careless.

17 A quick-tempered person acts foolishly,
and one who schemes is hated.

18 The inexperienced inherit foolishness,
but the sensible are crowned
with knowledge.

19 The evil bow before those who are good,
and the wicked, at the gates
of the righteous.

20 A poor person is hated even
by his neighbor,
but there are many who love the rich.

21 The one who despises his neighbor sins,
but whoever shows kindness to the poor
will be happy.

22 Don't those who plan evil go astray?
But those who plan good find loyalty
and faithfulness.

23 There is profit in all hard work,
but endless talk leads only to poverty.

24 The crown of the wise is their wealth,
but the foolishness of fools
produces foolishness.

25 A truthful witness rescues lives,
but one who utters lies is deceitful.

26 In the fear of the LORD one has
strong confidence
and his children have a refuge.

27 The fear of the LORD is a fountain of life,
turning people away from the snares
of death.

28 A large population is a king's splendor,
but a shortage of people is
a ruler's devastation.

29 A patient person shows great
understanding,
but a quick-tempered one
promotes foolishness.

30 A tranquil heart is life to the body,
but jealousy is rottenness to the bones.

31 The one who oppresses the poor person
insults his Maker,
but one who is kind to the needy
honors him.

32 The wicked one is thrown down
by his own sin,
but the righteous one has a refuge
in his death.

33 Wisdom resides in the heart
of the discerning;
she is known even among fools.

34 Righteousness exalts a nation,
but sin is a disgrace to any people.

35 A king favors a prudent servant,
but his anger falls on a disgraceful one.

Wound Up in This World

We live in a noisy world—constantly bombarded with things to get our attention, including social media, twenty-four-hour news cycles, endless sound bites from any and everyone. So giving focused attention to the vast issues that come with pursuing everlasting wisdom for everyday life is a challenge. We're wound up by opinions, decisions, and life events, often finding it difficult to turn our thoughts off long enough to actually hear from Jesus. But what if the Word of God was the first thing we heard each day? What if the Word of God was in our hearts as those sound bites bombard us? What if in our conversations with people, we also listened to what God might have to say to us?

Proverbs 14 says this would result in our being slow to anger. Hearing the wisdom of God's Word informs the way we hear and respond to others. As we become filled up with God's wisdom, we're less prone to get wound up by the world. The more we pause and seek to listen to God, the more our hearts are ready to do that with other people. As verses 17 and 29 teach us, patience makes way for wisdom and understanding, but a quick temper makes way for foolish schemes.

Without question, there is much in this noisy world that can turn our hearts toward anger. But this noisy world needs the hope of Jesus. Wisdom, then, reminds us to seek to hear from God more than we seek to be heard. Wisdom reminds us to marvel at the mystery of who God is more than we marvel at the problems or failures of other people. And as we respond to wisdom's reminders, we will set aside foolish anger so that we might patiently understand and embrace our greater role in His kingdom purposes.

How does listening to God's Word slow our anger toward people?

Read Proverbs 14:27 and 34. How do these verses speak to your role in God's kingdom purposes? How does anger impact these intended effects?

Seek to hear from God more than you seek to be heard.

WEEK 3

Growing in Wisdom Through Relationships

PROVERBS 15-21

Wisdom's Greatness

Here's a thought-provoking question as we begin week 3 of our study in Proverbs: Is your walk with the Lord good or is it great? In other words, would you say that God is doing "pretty good" things in you and through you, or is your life marked by *greatness*, as defined by God and given to you through His grace?

Now that we're halfway through the book of Proverbs, you're probably gaining some new understanding about that walk. To dig in a little deeper, though, consider Proverbs 18:16, which indicates that God uses our generosity to bring us the great things He has in store. That's a valuable piece of wisdom, but don't miss the greater reality. Our generosity, like every other wise behavior God calls us to, is not the origin of greatness in life. The starting point of greatness in life, the finishing point, and every point in between, is *God's generosity to us* in the life, death, and resurrection of Jesus Christ.

Greatness, then, isn't about any wise thing *we* do, in and of ourselves. It is about being connected to the Giver of all wisdom. It is a lifestyle defined by intimate connection to Jesus and other people who are also connected to Jesus.

We need the generous gifts of God's Word and God's people to grow in wisdom. God speaks wisdom to us through His Word and also through relationships with others. As we listen and put that wisdom into practice, He opens the door to move us from a good life to a great life where we receive the matchless blessing of participating in God's kingdom purposes.

Start

Use this page to introduce the idea and then get the conversation started.

Last week we learned that God speaks to us through His Word. How did God speak to you in your study of Proverbs 8–14?

This week, we'll be considering that wisdom isn't something we gain alone. God often uses others to point us toward His wisdom. Unfortunately, we often prefer to find answers on our own without asking for help from others. Think about how you typically seek out wisdom:

Is it easy or difficult for you to ask another person for help? Why is it sometimes hard for us to ask for help?

What is an area of life where you'd say you are teachable? In others words, in what situation do you readily seek out help and then apply that help? Now identify an area of life where you tend to try to handle problems on your own, without any outside help.

Prayer

Thank God for the gift of relationship with other believers.
Invite Him to strengthen and deepen those relationships
as a way of helping you grow in wisdom.

Watch

Use this page to take notes as you watch the group teaching session.

To access the teaching sessions,
use the instructions in the back
of your Bible study book.

Discuss

Use this section to discuss the video teaching.

Who is someone God has used to help you grow in wisdom? How so?

Vance pointed out that various verses in Proverbs teach us that "a wise way to live is to always seek input from others when making decisions." Why is that "always" true? (See Proverbs 11:14; 12:15; 13:10; 13:20; 15:22 for help.)

What challenges are there for us in seeking input from others when making decisions? Considering these challenges, why do you think God's plan is to grow us in wisdom through relationships with other people?

Vance gave the following three governing statements: "My input is never enough. My perspective is always limited. My flesh is always deceitful." What do these truths teach us about the everlasting wisdom God wants to give us?

We were given three "musts" in the video session: 1. Your relationships must include people you trust to speak God's wisdom into your life. 2. You must be willing to seek input from those that are in your life. 3. You must be teachable and listen to their input. Which of these three "musts" stands out to you the most? Why?

Practically speaking, how should each of those "musts" impact us in the day-to-day?

Do ongoing relationships with people who speak wisdom into your life help you with past decisions, present decisions, future decisions, or some mixture of the three? Explain.

It's not just about being wise or foolish; our decisions have far-reaching implications. We learned the following four impacts of unwise decision-making:

1. People get hurt.
2. Relationships get broken.
3. There are unintended consequences we didn't see coming.
4. Good intentions are wasted.

Considering these impacts, what does seeking input from others say about a person? What does *not* seeking input say about a person?

15

A gentle answer turns away anger,
but a harsh word stirs up wrath.

2 The tongue of the wise
makes knowledge attractive,
but the mouth of fools
blurts out foolishness.

3 The eyes of the LORD are everywhere,
observing the wicked and the good.

4 The tongue that heals is a tree of life,
but a devious tongue breaks the spirit.

5 A fool despises his father's discipline,
but a person who accepts correction
is sensible.

6 The house of the righteous
has great wealth,
but trouble accompanies the income
of the wicked.

7 The lips of the wise broadcast knowledge,
but not so the heart of fools.

8 The sacrifice of the wicked is detestable
to the LORD,
but the prayer of the upright is his delight.

9 The LORD detests the way of the wicked,
but he loves the one
who pursues righteousness.

10 Discipline is harsh for the one who leaves
the path;
the one who hates correction will die.

11 Sheol and Abaddon lie open
before the LORD—
how much more, human hearts.

12 A mocker doesn't love one
who corrects him;
he will not consult the wise.

13 A joyful heart makes a face cheerful,
but a sad heart produces a broken spirit.

14 A discerning mind seeks knowledge,
but the mouth of fools feeds
on foolishness.

15 All the days of the oppressed
are miserable,
but a cheerful heart has a continual feast.

16 Better a little with the fear of the LORD
than great treasure with turmoil.

17 Better a meal of vegetables
where there is love
than a fattened ox with hatred.

18 A hot-tempered person stirs up conflict,
but one slow to anger calms strife.

19 A slacker's way is like a thorny hedge,
but the path of the upright is a highway.

20 A wise son brings joy to his father,
but a foolish man despises his mother.

21 Foolishness brings joy to one
without sense,
but a person with understanding walks
a straight path.

22 Plans fail when there is no counsel,
but with many advisers they succeed.

23 A person takes joy in giving an answer;
and a timely word—how good that is!

24 For the prudent the path of life
leads upward,
so that he may avoid going down to Sheol.

25 The LORD tears apart the house
of the proud,
but he protects the widow's territory.

26 The LORD detests the plans of the one who
is evil,
but pleasant words are pure.

27 The one who profits dishonestly troubles
his household,
but the one who hates bribes will live.

28 The mind of the righteous person thinks
before answering,
but the mouth of the wicked blurts out
evil things.

29 The LORD is far from the wicked,
but he hears the prayer of the righteous.

30 Bright eyes cheer the heart;
good news strengthens the bones.

31 One who listens to life-giving rebukes
will be at home among the wise.

32 Anyone who ignores discipline
despises himself,
but whoever listens to correction acquires
good sense.

33 The fear of the LORD is what
wisdom teaches,
and humility comes before honor.

The Nuances of Words and Wisdom

There are many verses in Proverbs that instruct us about the wisdom we need in our words. In chapter 10, for instance, we read several verses that teach us to talk less and listen more so that we might receive correction and store up wisdom. Here in chapter 15, there are numerous other verses that specifically address our speech.

Verses 1 and 18 remind us that the delivery of our words can either cause anger or turn it away. Verses 2, 7, and 14 explain that the way we communicate can either invite discussion and knowledge or impart ignorance. Verses 4 and 23 teach us that our words can either encourage someone or break his or her spirit altogether. And verse 28 warns that we can either think and carefully speak words of righteousness or we can blurt out wickedness.

Besides the fact that our words matter and have great effect, we can sum up the wisdom of this instruction about words in this way—what we say is no less important than the way we say it. The nuances of communication are vast! We've all misinterpreted the heart of an email, text message, or social media post or had our words misinterpreted by someone else. Even in face-to-face conversations, we need to show wisdom in the way we speak. Our body language, expressions, tone, and timing all communicate a message that either invigorates the message of our actual words, confuses them, or diminishes them entirely. If we want to walk in wisdom, then, we must invite God to help us give careful attention to our words and how we communicate them.

Which of the verses about words in Proverbs 15 stands out to you the most? Why?

What does the fact that God want us to turn away anger, invite knowledge and discussion, encourage others, and speak words of righteousness teach you about His ultimate purpose for speech?

What we say is no less important than the way we say it.

16

The reflections of the heart
belong to mankind,
but the answer of the tongue is
from the Lord.

2 All a person's ways seem right to him,
but the Lord weighs motives.

3 Commit your activities to the Lord,
and your plans will be established.

4 The Lord has prepared everything
for his purpose—
even the wicked for the day of disaster.

5 Everyone with a proud heart is detestable
to the Lord;
be assured, he will not go unpunished.

6 Iniquity is atoned for by loyalty
and faithfulness,
and one turns from evil by the fear
of the Lord.

7 When a person's ways please the Lord,
he makes even his enemies to be at peace
with him.

8 Better a little with righteousness
than great income with injustice.

9 A person's heart plans his way,
but the Lord determines his steps.

10 God's verdict is on the lips of a king;
his mouth should not give
an unfair judgment.

11 Honest balances and scales are the Lord's;
all the weights in the bag are his concern.

12 Wicked behavior is detestable to kings,
since a throne is established
through righteousness.

13 Righteous lips are a king's delight,
and he loves one who speaks honestly.

14 A king's fury is a messenger of death,
but a wise person appeases it.

15 When a king's face lights up, there is life;
his favor is like a cloud with spring rain.

16 Get wisdom—
how much better it is than gold!
And get understanding—
it is preferable to silver.

17 The highway of the upright avoids evil;
the one who guards his way protects
his life.

18 Pride comes before destruction,
and an arrogant spirit before a fall.

19 Better to be lowly of spirit
with the humble
than to divide plunder with the proud.

20 The one who understands a matter
finds success,
and the one who trusts in the Lord
will be happy.

21 Anyone with a wise heart
is called discerning,
and pleasant speech increases learning.

22 Insight is a fountain of life
for its possessor,
but the discipline of fools is folly.

23 The heart of a wise person instructs
his mouth;
it adds learning to his speech.

24 Pleasant words are a honeycomb:
sweet to the taste and health to the body.

25 There is a way that seems right
to a person,
but its end is the way to death.

26 A worker's appetite works for him
because his hunger urges him on.

27 A worthless person digs up evil,
and his speech is like a scorching fire.

28 A contrary person spreads conflict,
and a gossip separates close friends.

29 A violent person lures his neighbor,
leading him on a path that is not good.

30 The one who narrows his eyes
is planning deceptions;
the one who compresses his lips
brings about evil.

31 Gray hair is a glorious crown;
it is found in the ways of righteousness.

32 Patience is better than power,
and controlling one's emotions,
than capturing a city.

33 The lot is cast into the lap,
but its every decision is from the Lord.

God-Given Foresight

Pride comes before the fall (Proverbs 16:18). We've heard it said a million times. Yet we often only remember this when we get to the point of actually falling! In hindsight, our pride becomes painfully obvious. In the destruction and stumbling, we see that pride led us there.

Tragically, God's people can lead the march on that road to destruction. We see it in Scripture and we see it in the lives of Christians today. But that only happens when we operate by human wisdom instead of God's wisdom. There is a way that seems right to us, but that way that seems right is wrong (v. 25).

Throughout Proverbs we see that we must choose God's way instead of our own. Left unchecked, pride causes us to think we know everything, so that we depend on ourselves as we make choices in our relationships, our work, and our words. Pride shapes our worldview. It prompts us to not listen to wisdom or receive it, believing we know ourselves the way to avoid dangers—or that we can figure it out along the way. In our pride, we want to earn a pat on the back from God and people. We hold up our good works and church attendance as if we have checked all of the boxes God desires for us.

The Lord knows all of this about us. He knows we are inclined to lean on our own abilities, contributions, and talents. And He has given us His Word so that we don't have to get to the point of hindsight before we recognize the danger of pride and our inclination toward it. He gives us foresight! His call to humility and dependence on Him is a call to life. It's a call to save us from destruction.

Circle every verse in Proverbs 16 that speaks to the problem of pride.

What is an area of life where you are tempted toward pridefulness? What does Proverbs 16 teach you about that?

Pride comes before the fall.

MONTH   DAY   YEAR

17

Better a dry crust with peace
than a house full of feasting with strife.

2 A prudent servant will rule over
   a disgraceful son
and share an inheritance among brothers.

3 A crucible for silver, and a smelter
   for gold,
and the Lord is the tester of hearts.

4 A wicked person listens to malicious talk;
a liar pays attention to
   a destructive tongue.

5 The one who mocks the poor insults
   his Maker,
and one who rejoices over calamity
will not go unpunished.

6 Grandchildren are the crown
   of the elderly,
and the pride of children is their fathers.

7 Eloquent words are not appropriate
   on a fool's lips;
how much worse are lies for a ruler.

8 A bribe seems like a magic stone
   to its owner;
wherever he turns, he succeeds.

9 Whoever conceals an offense
   promotes love,
but whoever gossips about it
   separates friends.

10 A rebuke cuts into a perceptive person
more than a hundred lashes into a fool.

11 An evil person desires only rebellion;
a cruel messenger will be sent
   against him.

12 Better for a person to meet a bear robbed
   of her cubs
than a fool in his foolishness.

13 If anyone returns evil for good,
evil will never depart from his house.

14 To start a conflict is to release a flood;
stop the dispute before it breaks out.

15 Acquitting the guilty and condemning
   the just—
both are detestable to the Lord.

16 Why does a fool have money in his hand
with no intention of buying wisdom?

17 A friend loves at all times,
and a brother is born for a difficult time.

18 One without sense enters an agreement
and puts up security for his friend.

19 One who loves to offend loves strife;
one who builds a high threshold
   invites injury.

20 One with a twisted mind will not succeed,
and one with deceitful speech will fall
   into ruin.

21 A man fathers a fool to his own sorrow;
the father of a fool has no joy.

22 A joyful heart is good medicine,
but a broken spirit dries up the bones.

23 A wicked person secretly takes a bribe
to subvert the course of justice.

24 Wisdom is the focus of the perceptive,
but a fool's eyes roam to the ends
   of the earth.

25 A foolish son is grief to his father
and bitterness to the one who bore him.

26 It is certainly not good to fine
   an innocent person
or to beat a noble for his honesty.

27 The one who has knowledge restrains
   his words,
and one who keeps a cool head
is a person of understanding.

28 Even a fool is considered wise
   when he keeps silent—
discerning, when he seals his lips.

Becoming Pursuers of Peace

Proverbs 17:1 makes it clear that the effects of peace and conflict in a person's life are a very big deal. So big, in fact, that it would be better to eat the leftover stale crust of an old, already eaten sandwich for dinner than to have an all-you-can-eat buffet if it means the difference between peace and conflict.

That doesn't mean that we should all just "live and let live," as the saying goes. The wisdom we read in God's Word is never void of truth. Notice how the wise pursuit of peace and reconciliation is described throughout chapter 17. It isn't about accepting all behaviors; it's about accepting behaviors that love God and people—at all times. Pursuers of peace don't give attention to malicious and destructive words that insult people and celebrate their adversity (vv. 4-5). They don't go around talking about what someone did wrong; they choose to forgive so they can move past it (v. 9). They don't look to start conflicts; they look to end them (v. 14). They don't love to take digs at someone else's expense; they love to step up to support someone in trouble (vv. 17,19). They don't quickly comment on everything they hear; they take time to listen and process before speaking (vv. 27-28).

Based on these principles, we must consider whether or not we are pursuing peace and reconciliation in our relationships. The effects of that answer are powerful and far-reaching. And in any relationship where conflict currently thrives, now is the perfect time to begin pursuing peace and reconciliation, instead.

Thinking back to Proverbs 16, why is it hard for us to pursue peace and reconciliation?

Are you pursuing peace and reconciliation in your relationships? What is a relationship you have where that is difficult? How does Proverbs 17 speak to you about that relationship?

Wisdom always pursues peace and reconciliation in relationships.

18 One who isolates himself pursues
selfish desires;
he rebels against all sound wisdom.

2 A fool does not delight
in understanding,
but only wants to show off
his opinions.

3 When a wicked person comes,
contempt also comes,
and along with dishonor, derision.

4 The words of a person's mouth
are deep waters,
a flowing river, a fountain
of wisdom.

5 It is not good to show partiality
to the guilty,
denying an innocent person justice.

6 A fool's lips lead to strife,
and his mouth provokes a beating.

7 A fool's mouth is his devastation,
and his lips are a trap for his life.

8 A gossip's words are like choice food
that goes down
to one's innermost being.

9 The one who is lazy in his work
is brother to a vandal.

10 The name of the Lord is
a strong tower;
the righteous run to it
and are protected.

11 The wealth of the rich is
his fortified city;
in his imagination it is
like a high wall.

12 Before his downfall a person's heart
is proud,
but humility comes before honor.

13 The one who gives an answer
before he listens —
this is foolishness and disgrace
for him.

14 A person's spirit can
endure sickness,
but who can survive a broken spirit?

15 The mind of the discerning
acquires knowledge,
and the ear of the wise seeks it.

16 A person's gift opens doors for him
and brings him before the great.

17 The first to state his case seems right
until another comes and cross-
examines him.

18 Casting the lot ends quarrels
and separates powerful opponents.

19 An offended brother is
harder to reach
than a fortified city,
and quarrels are like the bars
of a fortress.

20 From the fruit of a person's mouth
his stomach
is satisfied;
he is filled with the product
of his lips.

21 Death and life are in the power
of the tongue,
and those who love it will eat
its fruit.

22 A man who finds a wife finds
a good thing
and obtains favor from the Lord.

23 The poor person pleads,
but the rich one answers roughly.

24 One with many friends
may be harmed,
but there is a friend who stays closer
than a brother.

The Selfishness of Isolation

With all the warnings the book of Proverbs gives us about our words, we might think the best tact is to simply remove ourselves from relationships. If we don't engage with people, we won't get mad at them, right? We won't take digs at people, speak too quickly, gossip, or start even one conflict. As we read through chapter 18, the growing list continues. Engaging in relationships with people can tempt us to show off our opinions (v. 2), show partiality (v. 5), wrongly state our case (v. 17), carelessly answer a needy person (v. 23), and even provoke a beating (v. 6)! There is no doubt about it; relationships can cause trouble!

However, Proverbs 18:1 assures us that isolation isn't the answer. In fact, removing oneself entirely from community can be as destructive as surrounding oneself with people who make poor decisions. If left to ourselves, we will pursue selfish desires in every single context of life. We will, in effect, war against wisdom all by ourselves.

It's true that what we say matters, and we are often tempted to say wrong things. It's also true that how we live matters, and we are often tempted to live in ways that do not honor the Lord or show grace to other people the Lord has created. And it is precisely because of those truths that we need other people. God made us for relationship. We need the accountability of faithful friends to help us pursue godly wisdom.

Scripture instructs us to spend time alone with the Lord. What is the difference between seclusion and isolation?

God made you for relationship. How have you seen the benefits of community in your pursuit of wisdom? How have you seen the danger of isolation?

Removing ourselves from community is destructive.

19

Better a poor person who lives
with integrity
than someone who has deceitful lips
and is a fool.

2 Even zeal is not good without knowledge,
and the one who acts hastily sins.

3 A person's own foolishness leads
him astray,
yet his heart rages against the Lord.

4 Wealth attracts many friends,
but a poor person is separated
from his friend.

5 A false witness will not go unpunished,
and one who utters lies will not escape.

6 Many seek a ruler's favor,
and everyone is a friend of one
who gives gifts.

7 All the brothers of a poor person hate him;
how much more do his friends
keep their distance from him!
He may pursue them with words,
but they are not there.

8 The one who acquires good sense
loves himself;
one who safeguards understanding
finds success.

9 A false witness will not go unpunished,
and one who utters lies perishes.

10 Luxury is not appropriate for a fool —
how much less for a slave to rule
over princes!

11 A person's insight gives him patience,
and his virtue is to overlook an offense.

12 A king's rage is like the roaring of a lion,
but his favor is like dew on the grass.

13 A foolish son is his father's ruin,
and a wife's nagging is
an endless dripping.

14 A house and wealth are inherited
from fathers,
but a prudent wife is from the Lord.

15 Laziness induces deep sleep,
and a lazy person will go hungry.

16 The one who keeps commands
preserves himself;
one who disregards his ways will die.

17 Kindness to the poor is a loan to the Lord,
and he will give a reward to the lender.

18 Discipline your son while there is hope;
don't set your heart on being the cause
of his death.

19 A person with intense anger bears
the penalty;
if you rescue him, you'll have to do
it again.

20 Listen to counsel and receive instruction
so that you may be wise later in life.

21 Many plans are in a person's heart,
but the Lord's decree will prevail.

22 What is desirable in a person is
his fidelity;
better to be a poor person than a liar.

23 The fear of the Lord leads to life;
one will sleep at night without danger.

24 The slacker buries his hand in the bowl;
he doesn't even bring it back to his mouth!

25 Strike a mocker, and the inexperienced
learn a lesson;
rebuke the discerning,
and he gains knowledge.

26 The one who plunders his father
and evicts his mother
is a disgraceful and shameful son.

27 If you stop listening to correction, my son,
you will stray from the words
of knowledge.

28 A worthless witness mocks justice,
and a wicked mouth swallows iniquity.

29 Judgments are prepared for mockers,
and beatings for the backs of fools.

An Unhurried Pursuit

Anyone who has cared for an infant overnight knows we are not born patient. But it's not just in infancy that our impatience causes tension to arise in our lives. Not being able to have everything we want or need when we want or need it is part of living in a sinful world. The Bible is full of people who didn't want to wait on God, and we are no different. When life comes up against us, it is hard to be patient. When decisions need to be made, our default is to hurry that process. We want the decision to be made in a way that suits our preferences, and we want the decision to be made *now*.

Waiting on the Lord is a choice we learn to make as Jesus works in our lives to give us His wisdom. Proverbs 19:2 points out that impatience, or not waiting on God's wisdom, is a sin. And don't miss the first part of the verse—even zeal apart from the knowledge and belief that God is at work is foolish. In other words, we can be passionate about a choice we are making, but if we don't wait for the Lord, that passionate choice is a sin. Good and heartfelt intentions are no substitute for the wisdom and will of God.

As individuals, we can certainly identify times we rushed ahead of the Lord to our detriment. It happens collectively, too. We see this play out often in church life when we push forward in ministry decisions that seem right to us, even though we haven't waited for the Lord to speak into the situation. In effect, we adopt an "If we build it, He will come" type of mentality. And that's backwards. Proverbs reminds us to never act hastily but to patiently wait to hear from God—in all things.

What is the connection between daily time with the Lord and patience in decision-making?

What danger is there in rushing ahead of the Lord, thinking He will surely bless your good intentions? Where have you been tempted to do that?

Heartfelt intentions are no substitute for the wisdom and will of God.

20 Wine is a mocker, beer is a brawler;
whoever goes astray because of them
is not wise.

2 A king's terrible wrath is like the roaring
of a lion;
anyone who provokes him
endangers himself.

3 Honor belongs to the person who ends
a dispute,
but any fool can get himself into a quarrel.

4 The slacker does not plow
during planting season;
at harvest time he looks, and there is
nothing.

5 Counsel in a person's heart is deep water;
but a person of understanding
draws it out.

6 Many a person proclaims his own loyalty,
but who can find a trustworthy person?

7 A righteous person acts with integrity;
his children who come after him
will be happy.

8 A king sitting on a throne to judge
separates out all evil with his eyes.

9 Who can say, "I have kept my heart pure;
I am cleansed from my sin"?

10 Differing weights and varying measures—
both are detestable to the Lord.

11 Even a young man is known
by his actions—
by whether his behavior is pure
and upright.

12 The hearing ear and the seeing eye—
the Lord made them both.

13 Don't love sleep, or you will become poor;
open your eyes, and you'll have
enough to eat.

14 "It's worthless, it's worthless!"
the buyer says,
but after he is on his way, he gloats.

15 There is gold and a multitude of jewels,
but knowledgeable lips are a rare treasure.

16 Take his garment,
for he has put up security for a stranger;
get collateral if it is for foreigners.

17 Food gained by fraud is sweet to a person,
but afterward his mouth is full of gravel.

18 Finalize plans with counsel,
and wage war with sound guidance.

19 The one who reveals secrets is
a constant gossip;
avoid someone with a big mouth.

20 Whoever curses his father or mother—
his lamp will go out in deep darkness.

21 An inheritance gained prematurely
will not be blessed ultimately.

22 Don't say, "I will avenge this evil!"
Wait on the Lord, and he will rescue you.

23 Differing weights are detestable
to the Lord,
and dishonest scales are unfair.

24 Even a courageous person's steps
are determined
by the Lord,
so how can anyone understand
his own way?

25 It is a trap for anyone to dedicate
something rashly
and later to reconsider his vows.

26 A wise king separates out the wicked
and drives the threshing wheel over them.

27 The Lord's lamp sheds light on
a person's life,
searching the innermost parts.

28 Loyalty and faithfulness guard a king;
through loyalty he maintains his throne.

29 The glory of young men is their strength,
and the splendor of old men is gray hair.

30 Lashes and wounds purge away evil,
and beatings cleanse the innermost parts.

One Job

"You had one job" yields millions of results on an internet search. It's a common response to someone's failure to correctly do the simple task they set out to do. For example, the words "Turn Left" painted in large block letters in a right turn only lane.

We know we need to pass on wisdom to those who come behind us. At the same time, we often feel inept and unable to do that. We worry that the epitaph of our lives might speak more of failure than wisdom. Parents and grandparents know their roles have the power to illuminate feelings of ineptitude and inability more than anything else in life. Our failures can impact generations to come.

As Proverbs 20:7 assures us, so can walking in wisdom. The fact is, we will fail, and so will our children. So the happiness, or *blessedness* as other translations express it, does not come from raising "good kids" who make good decisions and stay out of trouble. It's about raising kids who know and follow the Lord, wanting His wisdom to shine light on their lives, even the parts no one else can see (v. 27). To do that, we must show the priority of relationship over rules. We must walk with the Lord in integrity, even when we mess up. To that end, we must trust God and join Him in opening the next generation's ears and eyes to wisdom (vv. 11-12).

To pass on a legacy of wisdom for generations to come, you don't have to do everything right. The reality is that there is only one job you have that ultimately matters, and that is to daily follow Jesus with your whole heart. When Christ is at the center, everything else will work itself out.

What are some pursuits our culture tends to think will bring happiness to children? What does Proverbs teach about where happiness is found?

What takeaway is there in Proverbs 20:7 for someone who hasn't had wisdom passed down to them?

Walking in wisdom impacts generations.

21

A king's heart is like channeled water
   in the LORD's hand:
He directs it wherever he chooses.

2 All a person's ways seem right to him,
   but the LORD weighs hearts.

3 Doing what is righteous and just
   is more acceptable to the LORD
       than sacrifice.

4 The lamp that guides the wicked —
   haughty eyes and an arrogant heart —
       is sin.

5 The plans of the diligent certainly lead
       to profit,
   but anyone who is reckless
       certainly becomes poor.

6 Making a fortune through a lying tongue
   is a vanishing mist, a pursuit of death.

7 The violence of the wicked
       sweeps them away
   because they refuse to act justly.

8 A guilty one's conduct is crooked,
   but the behavior of the innocent
       is upright.

9 Better to live on the corner of a roof
   than to share a house with a nagging wife.

10 A wicked person desires evil;
    he has no consideration for his neighbor.

11 When a mocker is punished,
    the inexperienced become wiser;
    when one teaches a wise man,
    he acquires knowledge.

12 The Righteous One considers the house
       of the wicked;
    he brings the wicked to ruin.

13 The one who shuts his ears to the cry
       of the poor
    will himself also call out
       and not be answered.

14 A secret gift soothes anger,
    and a covert bribe, fierce rage.

15 Justice executed is a joy to the righteous
    but a terror to evildoers.

16 The person who strays from the way
       of prudence
    will come to rest in the assembly of
       the departed spirits.

17 The one who loves pleasure
       will become poor;
    whoever loves wine and oil will not
       get rich.

18 The wicked are a ransom
       for the righteous,
    and the treacherous, for the upright.

19 Better to live in a wilderness
    than with a nagging
       and hot-tempered wife.

20 Precious treasure and oil are
       in the dwelling
       of a wise person,
    but a fool consumes them.

21 The one who pursues righteousness
       and faithful love
    will find life, righteousness, and honor.

22 A wise person went up against a city
       of warriors
    and brought down its secure fortress.

23 The one who guards his mouth
       and tongue
    keeps himself out of trouble.

24 The arrogant and proud person,
       named "Mocker,"
    acts with excessive arrogance.

25 A slacker's craving will kill him
    because his hands refuse to work.
26 He is filled with craving all day long,
    but the righteous give and don't
       hold back.

27 The sacrifice of a wicked person
       is detestable —
    how much more so
    when he brings it with ulterior motives!

28 A lying witness will perish,
    but the one who listens
       will speak successfully.

29 A wicked person puts on a bold face,
    but the upright one considers his way.

30 No wisdom, no understanding,
       and no counsel
    will prevail against the LORD.

31 A horse is prepared for the day of battle,
    but victory comes from the LORD.

Who God Is

Our culture increasingly operates under the assumption that respect isn't something automatically given, it must be earned. This way of thinking impacts our view of authority and how we respond to those who have authority over us. We question them (at least in thought), at every turn.

Proverbs 21 teaches numerous truths about God that relate to the issues of respect and authority. He is in complete control (v. 1). He sees our motives clearly (v. 2). Righteousness and justice are His priority (v. 3). He will undo wickedness (v. 12). His wisdom will never be outmatched by anyone or anything (v. 30). He will bring victory (v. 31).

Proverbs doesn't only give wisdom about how we are to live each day; it gives wisdom about who God is. When we truly understand who God is, everything about who we understand ourselves to be changes—including how we relate to other people. How we respond to authority, then, is a reflection of who we believe God to be.

Verse 1 assures us that God is the ultimate authority. He has authority over the human heart and the human will. His authority remains secure, even when human authority exerts itself in sinful ways. All people, even the kings of this world, are under God's power and rule, and, ultimately, He will have His way. Our respect and submission to authority, then, is respect for the Lord and submission to Him.

Circle every verse that speaks to the character and qualities of God. Which stands out to you the most? Why?

What authorities in your life are difficult for you to respond to wisely? How does Proverbs 21:1 encourage you in that?

How we respond to authority is a reflection of who we believe God to be.

WEEK 4

Walking in Wisdom

Through Life

PROVERBS 22-31

Wisdom's Legacy

In the past three weeks of study, you've undoubtedly seen that Proverbs provides wisdom for every area of life at every stage of life. As you've been gaining that wisdom, you've also been seeing life from God's perspective. That provision of wisdom and perspective isn't meant to end when you finish this workbook! God intends for you to continue searching out His wisdom each and every day of your life. God's wisdom is inexhaustible—but the pursuit of His wisdom is not *exhausting*; it is invigorating!

God's wisdom is a gift to us. He freely gives us His Word as a way to pursue Him. He wants us to experience and enjoy life to the fullest, and He gives us the wisdom of His Word for that purpose.

What we'll see in these remaining ten chapters of Proverbs is the fullness of life in God's wisdom and perspective extends far beyond ourselves. This gift we continue to receive from God isn't only meant to impact us; it impacts other people, too. We're meant to raise up the next generation in wisdom (22:6) with trusted friends, together leveraging the wisdom we have received to benefit others (24:10-12; 27:17). The application of God's wisdom in our personal lives—enjoying life to the fullest—leaves a legacy for others to receive, recognize, and celebrate (31:28-31).

God's everlasting wisdom for everyday life is for everyone, and He wants you to partner with Him in the fulfillment of that purpose. What a gift! Receive God's wisdom, enjoy life to the fullest, and leave a legacy as you do.

Start

Use this page to introduce the idea and then get the conversation started.

How has God used His Word and your relationships this week to help you grow in wisdom?

The pursuit of wisdom is not a short-term effort. Wisdom is worth pursuing throughout our entire lives. We can never master God's wisdom and are in constant need of learning to live out His wisdom and ways. Think about your experience with wisdom to this point in your life.

In your life, has growing in wisdom been more like an occasional event, a fruitful season, or a lifelong journey? Explain.

Do you think of yourself as someone who will leave a spiritual legacy to others? Explain.

Prayer

Thank God for the legacy of wisdom that He has freely given to you. Ask Him to continue the journey of growing in wisdom and to help you pass that legacy of wisdom on to others.

Watch

Use this page to take notes as you watch the group teaching session.

To access the teaching sessions,
use the instructions in the back
of your Bible study book.

Discuss

Use this section to discuss the video teaching.

We learned five closing truths in today's video teaching:

1. Wisdom is essential to enjoying all that life has to offer.
2. Wisdom doesn't come naturally.
3. Wisdom begins in time spent with God.
4. Wisdom is a journey, not a destination.
5. God desires to give you wisdom more than you desire to pursue it.

Which of these five truths do you sometimes struggle to believe? Why?

How would you counsel someone who makes foolish decisions, believing God's commands only prevent us from living our best lives?

Read Proverbs 16:16. Was the writer of this proverb using hyperbole? How is wisdom better than gold and silver?

Read Proverbs 20:9. How should we understand the journey of growing in wisdom? How should we respond when we mess up?

Vance told the story of "The Saddle Ridge Hoard," a treasure of gold coins found on private property in 2013 that was assessed to be worth over ten million dollars. The property owners had walked past those coins numerous times, without ever recognizing or receiving the treasure.

Why do we so often "walk past" the treasure chest of God's wisdom that is available to us?

What would your life be like if your pattern was to walk right past the treasure chest of God's wisdom in His Word and in relationships?

Now imagine that your pattern was to engage with God daily in the journey of growing in wisdom through His Word and relationships. Contrast that type of life with the previous scenario.

What choice do you have in those two very different outcomes?

Read James 1:5. Consider this verse in the context of the five closing truths. What should you do if you lack wisdom?

22

A good name is to be chosen
over great wealth;
favor is better than silver and gold.

2 Rich and poor have this in common:
the LORD makes them all.

3 A sensible person sees danger
and takes cover,
but the inexperienced keep going
and are punished.

4 Humility, the fear of the LORD,
results in wealth, honor, and life.

5 There are thorns and snares on the way
of the crooked;
the one who guards himself stays
far from them.

6 Start a youth out on his way;
even when he grows old he will not depart
from it.

7 The rich rule over the poor,
and the borrower is a slave to the lender.

8 The one who sows injustice
will reap disaster,
and the rod of his fury will be destroyed.

9 A generous person will be blessed,
for he shares his food with the poor.

10 Drive out a mocker, and conflict goes too;
then quarreling and dishonor will cease.

11 The one who loves a pure heart
and gracious lips—the king is his friend.

12 The LORD's eyes keep watch
over knowledge,
but he overthrows the words
of the treacherous.

13 The slacker says, "There's a lion outside!
I'll be killed in the public square!"

14 The mouth of the forbidden woman is
a deep pit;
a man cursed by the LORD will fall into it.

15 Foolishness is bound to the heart
of a youth;
a rod of discipline will separate it
from him.

16 Oppressing the poor to enrich oneself,
and giving to the rich—both lead
only to poverty.

WORDS OF THE WISE

17 Listen closely, pay attention to the words
of the wise,
and apply your mind to my knowledge.

18 For it is pleasing if you keep them
within you
and if they are constantly on your lips.

19 I have instructed you today—even you—
so that your confidence may be
in the LORD.

20 Haven't I written for you thirty sayings
about counsel and knowledge,

21 in order to teach you true
and reliable words,
so that you may give a dependable report
to those who sent you?

22 Don't rob a poor person
because he is poor,
and don't crush the oppressed at
the city gate,

23 for the LORD will champion their cause
and will plunder those who plunder them.

24 Don't make friends with an angry person,
and don't be a companion
of a hot-tempered one,

25 or you will learn his ways
and entangle yourself in a snare.

26 Don't be one of those
who enter agreements,
who put up security for loans.

27 If you have nothing with which to pay,
even your bed will be taken
from under you.

28 Don't move an ancient boundary marker
that your ancestors set up.

29 Do you see a person skilled in his work?
He will stand in the presence of kings.
He will not stand in the presence
of the unknown.

Equipping the Next Generation

What is something someone taught you when you were young that you still remember? Maybe it was something simple like scrambling eggs or doing laundry, or a bigger task like driving a car or doing your taxes. It is often the "small stuff" that sticks with us the longest. The younger we learn, the more ingrained these things become as we get older. The same is true in relationship with the Lord. The younger people are when they start learning God's wisdom, the more ready they are to walk in truth for a lifetime. And it is up to all of us to impart that wisdom to them.

Proverbs 22:6 indicates this is precisely why Proverbs was written. Solomon and others understood the responsibility of equipping future generations with the truth and knowledge of everlasting wisdom for everyday life. They wanted those who came after them to be filled with confidence in the Lord (vv. 17-21). Introducing someone to God, teaching them the truths of the gospel, and helping them be obedient to the work of the Spirit are high and holy responsibilities. And that wisdom goes beyond our words. The next generation is observant! They will watch to see how we live out God's wisdom in daily life. What we say should match what we do.

At the same time, Proverbs 22:6 isn't an assurance that if we invest in raising up the next generation in God's wisdom they won't ever veer off course. Every person who is taught God's wisdom may not choose to follow that wisdom. Our job is to steward God's wisdom well to the next generation, and trust Him to do the work that only He can do in their hearts.

What are some of the most significant wisdom principles you learned when you were young? Who taught you that wisdom? Why?

How does God use even our flaws to enable us to impart wisdom to the next generation?

It is up to all of us to impart wisdom to the next generation.

MONTH	DAY	YEAR

23

When you sit down to dine with a ruler,
consider carefully what is before you,
2 and put a knife to your throat
if you have a big appetite;
3 don't desire his choice food,
for that food is deceptive.

4 Don't wear yourself out to get rich;
because you know better, stop!
5 As soon as your eyes fly to it,
it disappears,
for it makes wings for itself
and flies like an eagle to the sky.

6 Don't eat a stingy person's bread,
and don't desire his choice food,
7 for it's like someone calculating inwardly.
"Eat and drink," he says to you,
but his heart is not with you.
8 You will vomit the little you've eaten
and waste your pleasant words.

9 Don't speak to a fool,
for he will despise the insight
of your words.

10 Don't move an ancient boundary marker,
and don't encroach on the fields
of the fatherless,
11 for their Redeemer is strong,
and he will champion their cause
against you.

12 Apply yourself to discipline
and listen to words of knowledge.

13 Don't withhold discipline from a youth;
if you punish him with a rod,
he will not die.
14 Punish him with a rod,
and you will rescue his life from Sheol.

15 My son, if your heart is wise,
my heart will indeed rejoice.
16 My innermost being will celebrate
when your lips say what is right.

17 Don't let your heart envy sinners;
instead, always fear the LORD.
18 For then you will have a future,
and your hope will not be dashed.

19 Listen, my son, and be wise;
keep your mind on the right course.
20 Don't associate with those who drink
too much wine
or with those who gorge themselves
on meat.
21 For the drunkard and the glutton
will become poor,
and grogginess will clothe them in rags.

22 Listen to your father who gave you life,
and don't despise your mother
when she is old.
23 Buy—and do not sell—truth,
wisdom, instruction, and understanding.
24 The father of a righteous son
will rejoice greatly,
and one who fathers a wise son
will delight in him.
25 Let your father and mother have joy,
and let her who gave birth to you rejoice.

26 My son, give me your heart,
and let your eyes observe my ways.
27 For a prostitute is a deep pit,
and a wayward woman is a narrow well;
28 indeed, she sets an ambush like a robber
and increases the number
of unfaithful people.

29 Who has woe? Who has sorrow?
Who has conflicts? Who has complaints?
Who has wounds for no reason?
Who has red eyes?
30 Those who linger over wine;
those who go looking for mixed wine.
31 Don't gaze at wine because it is red,
because it gleams in the cup
and goes down smoothly.
32 In the end it bites like a snake
and stings like a viper.
33 Your eyes will see strange things,
and you will say absurd things.
34 You'll be like someone sleeping out at sea
or lying down on the top of a ship's mast.
35 "They struck me, but I feel no pain!
They beat me, but I didn't know it!
When will I wake up?
I'll look for another drink."

Stop and Think

One of the wisdom principles seen throughout Proverbs is clearly expressed at the start of chapter 23—"Consider carefully." And continuing throughout this chapter, Solomon exhorts us to stop and think about the choices before us each and every day. Whether making choices that involve influential people (vv. 1-3), wealth (vv. 4-5), relationships with unwise people (vv. 6-9,17-18,20-21,27-28), or where we focus our attention (vv. 12,19,22-26,31-35), our appetites are big. As such, hasty decisions lead to foolish behavior.

The questions our choices present can be endless, and they feed the ravenous discontent within us. Solomon knew the emptiness and frustration of discontentment all too well. When he penned the words of Proverbs 23:4, he was reflecting back on his own experience of chasing the temporary pleasures of this world. Through that experience he learned the value of careful consideration.

Careful consideration of God's wisdom compels us to set aside temporary pleasures to invest instead in eternal things. As we stop and think about God's wisdom, we recognize He is our source and provider, caring for every detail of our lives. We remember the temporary nature of our earthly appetites. The feelings associated with those big appetites are also temporary. Any benefits we may think they offer are not worth the cost of foolish decisions. But the benefit of carefully considering God's wisdom is certain and valuable forever—He refocuses our minds and hearts on eternal things.

What is an area of life where you tend to focus on temporary circumstances instead of eternal truths? How does Proverbs 23 speak to you about that?

What would it mean, practically, for you to carefully consider God's wisdom in all things this week?

Careful consideration of wisdom compels us to invest in the eternal.

MONTH   DAY   YEAR

24

Don't envy the evil
or desire to be with them,
2   for their hearts plan violence,
and their words stir up trouble.

3   A house is built by wisdom,
and it is established by understanding;
4   by knowledge the rooms are filled
with every precious
and beautiful treasure.

5   A wise warrior is better than a strong one,
and a man of knowledge than one
of strength;
6   for you should wage war
with sound guidance —
victory comes with many counselors.

7   Wisdom is inaccessible to a fool;
he does not open his mouth
at the city gate.

8   The one who plots evil
will be called a schemer.
9   A foolish scheme is sin,
and a mocker is detestable to people.

10 If you do nothing in a difficult time,
your strength is limited.
11 Rescue those being taken off to death,
and save those stumbling
toward slaughter.
12 If you say, "But we didn't know
about this,"
won't he who weighs hearts consider it?
Won't he who protects your life know?
Won't he repay a person according to
his work?

13 Eat honey, my son, for it is good,
and the honeycomb is sweet
to your palate;
14 realize that wisdom is the same for you.
If you find it, you will have a future,
and your hope will never fade.

15 Don't set an ambush, you wicked one,
at the camp of the righteous man;
don't destroy his dwelling.
16 Though a righteous person falls
seven times,
he will get up,
but the wicked will stumble into ruin.

17 Don't gloat when your enemy falls,
and don't let your heart rejoice
when he stumbles,
18 or the Lord will see, be displeased,
and turn his wrath away from him.

19 Don't be agitated by evildoers,
and don't envy the wicked.
20 For the evil have no future;
the lamp of the wicked will be put out.

21 My son, fear the Lord, as well as the king,
and don't associate with rebels,
22 for destruction will come suddenly
from them;
who knows what distress these two
can bring?

23 These sayings also belong to the wise:

It is not good to show partiality
in judgment.
24 Whoever says to the guilty,
"You are innocent" —
peoples will curse him, and nations
will denounce him;
25 but it will go well with those who convict
the guilty,
and a generous blessing will come
to them.

26 He who gives an honest answer
gives a kiss on the lips.

27 Complete your outdoor work, and prepare
your field;
afterward, build your house.

28 Don't testify against your neighbor
without cause.
Don't deceive with your lips.
29 Don't say, "I'll do to him what he did
to me;
I'll repay the man for what he has done."

30 I went by the field of a slacker
and by the vineyard of one lacking sense.
31 Thistles had come up everywhere,
weeds covered the ground,
and the stone wall was ruined.
32 I saw, and took it to heart;
I looked, and received instruction:
33 a little sleep, a little slumber,
a little folding of the arms to rest,
34 and your poverty will come like a robber,
and your need, like a bandit.

On Mission

What is a skill or some knowledge you have used to benefit others? Architects use their skills to design houses for families and buildings for businesses to function efficiently. Moms and dads use their instincts and knowledge to keep children safe. Firefighters use their knowledge to extinguish threatening fires. Educators pass their knowledge on to students. Doctors use their knowledge to help sick people get well.

Proverbs 24 reminds us that God has called us to live on mission, wisely leveraging the skills and knowledge He has given us to benefit others. To do that, we must not join with people whose hearts are aimed at trouble (v. 1). Instead, we must partner with wise warriors whose hearts are aimed at living out God's mission in the world (vv. 5-6). As we do, we must boldly speak God's wisdom. To not contribute wisdom when given opportunity is foolish (v. 7). There are needs all around us, and God intends for us to live in a way that offers help to those who are hurting. We may be tempted to do nothing, but we can't live on mission if we don't speak and act on behalf of those in need of rescue (vv. 10-12). Where laziness and carelessness abound, so does trouble (vv. 30-34).

All believers in Jesus Christ have been sent into the world to carry out His mission. To do that, He gives us truth in His Word. He gives us skills and passions. He gives us fellowship with other believers who are also living on mission. And He places us in jobs and communities where there are needs. Wisdom looks for the opportunities to use those unique gifts in those specific places to rescue those who are perishing.

What is the connection between Proverbs 24:11 and Mark 16:15-16?

Name one way you can leverage your job, skills, or passions where you work, live, and play on mission this week.

God has called us to live on mission.

MONTH   DAY   YEAR

HEZEKIAH'S COLLECTION

25 These too are proverbs of Solomon,
which the men of King Hezekiah of Judah
copied.

2 It is the glory of God to conceal a matter
and the glory of kings to investigate
a matter.
3 As the heavens are high and the earth
is deep,
so the hearts of kings cannot
be investigated.

4 Remove impurities from silver,
and material will be produced
for a silversmith.
5 Remove the wicked
from the king's presence,
and his throne will be established
in righteousness.

6 Don't boast about yourself
before the king,
and don't stand in the place of the great;
7 for it is better for him to say to you,
"Come up here!"
than to demote you in plain view
of a noble.

8 Don't take a matter to court hastily.
Otherwise, what will you do afterward
if your opponent humiliates you?
9 Make your case with your opponent
without revealing another's secret;
10 otherwise, the one who hears
will disgrace you,
and you'll never live it down.

11 A word spoken at the right time
is like gold apples in silver settings.
12 A wise correction to a receptive ear
is like a gold ring or an ornament of gold.

13 To those who send him,
a trustworthy envoy
is like the coolness of snow
on a harvest day;
he refreshes the life of his masters.

14 The one who boasts about a gift
that does not exist
is like clouds and wind without rain.
15 A ruler can be persuaded
through patience,
and a gentle tongue can break a bone.
16 If you find honey, eat only what you need;
otherwise, you'll get sick from it
and vomit.
17 Seldom set foot in your neighbor's house;
otherwise, he'll get sick of you
and hate you.

18 A person giving false testimony
against his neighbor
is like a club, a sword, or a sharp arrow.
19 Trusting an unreliable person in a
difficult time
is like a rotten tooth or a faltering foot.

20 Singing songs to a troubled heart
is like taking off clothing on a cold day
or like pouring vinegar on soda.

21 If your enemy is hungry, give him food
to eat,
and if he is thirsty, give him water
to drink,
22 for you will heap burning coals
on his head,
and the LORD will reward you.

23 The north wind produces rain,
and a backbiting tongue, angry looks.

24 Better to live on the corner of a roof
than to share a house with a nagging wife.

25 Good news from a distant land
is like cold water to a parched throat.

26 A righteous person who yields
to the wicked
is like a muddied spring or a polluted well.

27 It is not good to eat too much honey
or to seek glory after glory.

28 A person who does not control his temper
is like a city whose wall is broken down.

Promise Keeper

Proverbs 25 covers some weighty topics—justice in government (v. 5), the foolishness of pride (vv. 6-7), what to do when you want to sue someone (vv. 8-10), giving false testimony (v. 18), and how to respond to your enemies (vv. 21-22), just to name a few. We might be tempted to take verse 14 less seriously when compared with the other issues in this chapter. After all, breaking a promise can't be as serious as wickedness in government or spreading lies about your neighbor, right?

If we tend to think that way, it is likely because we live in a low-commitment culture. We like to keep our options open, just in case something better comes along or our desires change. From event invites to relationships, we notoriously choose "maybe," wait until the last minute to decide, or we simply agree as a show of good intentions and then later back out on people.

This is no less common in the church. We might commit to a small group or area of service, but if we get too busy, those are often the first to go. We might commit to praying for someone, but the days get away from us and we forget. The thing is, we may live in a low-commitment culture, but we serve a high-commitment God. He wants us to say what we mean and mean what we say. That's because when we overpromise and under-deliver, we do not honor God and others as we ought.

Carelessness with words reveals a lack of integrity and a lack of attention to walking in wisdom. If we claim to know the truth of God, as it has been revealed in Jesus, and we claim to share that truth with the world, then we should be truthful to our own word. We make our promises and commitments to people before God.

What do we communicate to other people when we fail to keep our word?

What do we communicate to God when we make promises that we do not keep?

Say what you mean and mean what you say.

MONTH	DAY	YEAR

26 Like snow in summer and rain
at harvest,
honor is inappropriate for a fool.

2 Like a flitting sparrow
or a fluttering swallow,
an undeserved curse goes nowhere.
3 A whip for the horse, a bridle
for the donkey,
and a rod for the backs of fools.
4 Don't answer a fool according to
his foolishness
or you'll be like him yourself.
5 Answer a fool according to
his foolishness
or he'll become wise in his own eyes.
6 The one who sends a message
by a fool's hand
cuts off his own feet
and drinks violence.
7 A proverb in the mouth of a fool
is like lame legs that hang limp.
8 Giving honor to a fool
is like binding a stone in a sling.
9 A proverb in the mouth of a fool
is like a stick with thorns,
brandished by the hand
of a drunkard.
10 The one who hires a fool
or who hires those passing by
is like an archer
who wounds everyone
indiscriminately.
11 As a dog returns to its vomit,
so also a fool repeats his foolishness.
12 Do you see a person who is wise
in his own eyes?
There is more hope for a fool
than for him.

13 The slacker says, "There's a lion
in the road —
a lion in the public square!"
14 A door turns on its hinges,
and a slacker, on his bed.
15 The slacker buries his hand
in the bowl;
he is too weary to bring it
to his mouth!
16 In his own eyes, a slacker is wiser
than seven who can answer sensibly.

17 A person who is passing by and
meddles in a quarrel that's not his
is like one who grabs a dog
by the ears.
18 Like a madman who throws
flaming darts
and deadly arrows,
19 so is the person who deceives
his neighbor
and says, "I was only joking!"

20 Without wood, fire goes out;
without a gossip, conflict dies down.
21 As charcoal for embers and wood
for fire,
so is a quarrelsome person
for kindling strife.
22 A gossip's words are like choice food
that goes down to
one's innermost being.

23 Smooth lips with an evil heart
are like glaze on an earthen vessel.
24 A hateful person disguises himself
with his speech
and harbors deceit within.
25 When he speaks graciously,
don't believe him,
for there are seven detestable things
in his heart.
26 Though his hatred is concealed
by deception,
his evil will be revealed
in the assembly.
27 The one who digs a pit will fall
into it,
and whoever rolls a stone —
it will come back on him.
28 A lying tongue hates
those it crushes,
and a flattering mouth causes ruin.

Applying Wisdom with Wisdom

As we've been reading through Proverbs, we've received God's everlasting wisdom for everyday life. Some aspects of that wisdom give clear boundaries in every circumstance—trust God's wisdom, not your own (1:7; 2:3; 3:5); don't choose to take the way of wickedness (4:14); guard your heart (4:23); enjoy marriage and avoid seduction (5); live with integrity (10:9). There are other aspects of God's wisdom, though, that we must continue to seek out and carefully consider, depending on the circumstance.

For instance, Proverbs 26:4-5 teaches us that sometimes we should not answer a foolish person, and other times we should. We have also learned that we should rescue those in need and will be held accountable for our decisions in those situations (24:10-12). Yet here in Proverbs 26:17, we find there are instances where meddling in other's business might be pure foolishness. Sometimes wisdom minds its own business, and other times it takes on someone else's need as its business.

There are situations where there are no hard and fast rules for us to follow. This is precisely the reason why we must seek God's wisdom everyday. Wisdom approaches difficult situations with complete trust in the Lord, inviting Him to guide our thoughts, words, and behavior so that He might be glorified always, even in situations where the wise answer is not immediately clear.

What is a situation where you should not "answer a fool according to his foolishness" (v. 4)? What is a situation where you should (v. 5)?

What is a situation where you should not "meddle in a quarrel" (17)? What is a situation where you should?

The wise answer is not always immediately clear.

27 Don't boast about tomorrow,
for you don't know what a day
might bring.

2 Let another praise you, and not
your own mouth—
a stranger, and not your own lips.

3 A stone is heavy, and sand a burden,
but aggravation from a fool
outweighs them both.

4 Fury is cruel, and anger a flood,
but who can withstand jealousy?

5 Better an open reprimand
than concealed love.

6 The wounds of a friend
are trustworthy,
but the kisses of an enemy
are excessive.

7 A person who is full tramples
on a honeycomb,
but to a hungry person,
any bitter thing is sweet.

8 Anyone wandering from his home
is like a bird wandering from its nest.

9 Oil and incense bring joy
to the heart,
and the sweetness of a friend
is better
than self-counsel.

10 Don't abandon your friend
or your father's friend,
and don't go to your brother's house
in your time of calamity;
better a neighbor nearby
than a brother far away.

11 Be wise, my son, and bring
my heart joy,
so that I can answer anyone
who taunts me.

12 A sensible person sees danger
and takes cover;
the inexperienced keep going
and are punished.

13 Take his garment,
for he has put up security
for a stranger;
get collateral if it is for foreigners.

14 If one blesses his neighbor
with a loud voice early
in the morning,
it will be counted as a curse to him.

15 An endless dripping on a rainy day
and a nagging wife are alike;
16 the one who controls her controls
the wind
and grasps oil with his right hand.

17 Iron sharpens iron,
and one person sharpens another.

18 Whoever tends a fig tree will eat
its fruit,
and whoever looks after his master
will be honored.

19 As water reflects the face,
so the heart reflects the person.

20 Sheol and Abaddon are
never satisfied,
and people's eyes are never satisfied.
21 As a crucible refines silver,
and a smelter refines gold,
so a person should refine his praise.

22 Though you grind a fool
in a mortar with a pestle
along with grain,
you will not separate his foolishness
from him.

23 Know well the condition
of your flock,
and pay attention to your herds,
24 for wealth is not forever;
not even a crown lasts for all time.
25 When hay is removed
and new growth appears
and the grain from the hills
is gathered in,
26 lambs will provide your clothing,
and goats, the price of a field;
27 there will be enough goat's milk
for your food—
food for your household
and nourishment for your
female servants.

The Best Kind of Friends

The wisdom we find in Proverbs is all about relationships—relationships with God and people. That's because we were made for those relationships. God has designed us to be in relationship with Him and other people. But as we walk in those relationships, we are tempted every day to deviate from that design.

The way we most clearly see that deviation is when feelings and actions in those relationships go wrong. We encounter aggravation (27:3), anger, jealousy (v. 4), betrayal (v. 10), and nagging (v. 15). And certainly God's design is for us to relate to Him and others in love and unity. At the same time, Proverbs 27 emphasizes another aspect of God's relational design that we sometimes overlook or dismiss altogether—we need friends we can trust to mete out wisdom and we need to be the kind of friend who can be trusted to do the same.

Because the wise answer is not always clear, and because we do not always choose the wise way, we need friends who will help us. By God's design, those relationships are meant to give us open reprimand when needed (v. 5), speak truth into our lives even when it hurts (v. 6), and "sharpen" us so that we might walk in everlasting wisdom for everyday life (v. 17). This does not automatically occur, though. What occurs more often and most naturally is the foolishness of aggravation, anger, jealousy, betrayal, and nagging. To have the best kind of friends, who seek and apply God's wisdom, we must seek to be that kind of friend.

Based on Proverbs 27, what type of friendships does God intend for you to have?

What about that kind of friendship is difficult for you to give or receive? Why?

We need friends who help us walk in God's wisdom.

28

The wicked flee when no one
is pursuing them,
but the righteous are as bold as a lion.

2 When a land is in rebellion, it has
many rulers,
but with a discerning
and knowledgeable person,
it endures.

3 A destitute leader who oppresses the poor
is like a driving rain that leaves no food.

4 Those who reject the law
praise the wicked,
but those who keep the law pit themselves
against them.

5 The evil do not understand justice,
but those who seek the Lord
understand everything.

6 Better the poor person who lives
with integrity
than the rich one who distorts right
and wrong.

7 A discerning son keeps the law,
but a companion of gluttons humiliates
his father.

8 Whoever increases his wealth
through excessive interest
collects it for one who is kind to the poor.

9 Anyone who turns his ear
away from hearing the law—
even his prayer is detestable.

10 The one who leads the upright
into an evil way
will fall into his own pit,
but the blameless will inherit
what is good.

11 A rich person is wise in his own eyes,
but a poor one who has discernment
sees through him.

12 When the righteous triumph,
there is great rejoicing,
but when the wicked come to power,
people hide.

13 The one who conceals his sins
will not prosper,
but whoever confesses
and renounces them
will find mercy.

14 Happy is the one who is always reverent,
but one who hardens his heart falls
into trouble.

15 A wicked ruler over a helpless people
is like a roaring lion or a charging bear.

16 A leader who lacks understanding
is very oppressive,
but one who hates dishonest profit
prolongs his life.

17 Someone burdened by bloodguilt
will be a fugitive until death.
Let no one help him.

18 The one who lives with integrity
will be helped,
but one who distorts right and wrong
will suddenly fall.

19 The one who works his land
will have plenty of food,
but whoever chases fantasies
will have his fill of poverty.

20 A faithful person will have
many blessings,
but one in a hurry to get rich
will not go unpunished.

21 It is not good to show partiality—
yet even a courageous person may sin
for a piece of bread.

22 A greedy one is in a hurry for wealth;
he doesn't know that poverty will come
to him.

23 One who rebukes a person will later find
more favor
than one who flatters with his tongue.

24 The one who robs his father or mother
and says, "That's no sin,"
is a companion to a person who destroys.

25 A greedy person stirs up conflict,
but whoever trusts in the Lord
will prosper.

26 The one who trusts in himself is a fool,
but one who walks in wisdom
will be safe.

27 The one who gives to the poor
will not be in need,
but one who turns his eyes away
will receive many curses.

28 When the wicked come to power,
people hide,
but when they are destroyed,
the righteous flourish.

Kingdom Prayers

Sin blinds us. It is as simple as that. It dulls our senses and our ability to see God's wisdom. Proverbs 28:5 teaches that sin blinds us to the brokenness and injustice all around us. To walk in God's everlasting wisdom every day, we need sight and understanding only the Spirit of God can give.

Of course, Proverbs 28:5 doesn't mean believers understand everything in this life—that is impossible in our humanity. Even though we have the Spirit of God living and moving within us, we are limited by our flesh. But when we choose to follow Jesus, it changes the way we see the world. We begin to see life with a vision for the kingdom of God.

Seeing life with a vision for God's kingdom changes the way we pray. When we turn our hearts and minds to seek His wisdom, our prayers begin to align with that wisdom (v. 9). The way we engage with broken people and places, then, is radically changed as we join with Jesus in His power to redeem all things.

It also radically changes the way we see ourselves as we pray. We no longer want to hide from God. Instead, we become honest about our sins (v. 13). We acknowledge our foolishness to the Lord, trusting Him completely for mercy and restoration. Sin blinds us to the needs around us and the need of our own sinful hearts, but wisdom opens our eyes to pray and act in accordance with God's will.

Where do you need God to give you vision and understanding? How does that inform the way you pray?

Is confession a regular part of your prayer life? In terms of everlasting wisdom for everyday life, why should it be?

Seeing life with a vision for God's kingdom changes the way we pray.

29 One who becomes stiff-necked,
after many reprimands
will be shattered instantly—
beyond recovery.

2 When the righteous flourish,
the people rejoice,
but when the wicked rule, people groan.

3 A man who loves wisdom brings joy
to his father,
but one who consorts with prostitutes
destroys his wealth.

4 By justice a king brings stability to a land,
but a person who demands
"contributions"
demolishes it.

5 A person who flatters his neighbor
spreads a net for his feet.

6 An evil person is caught by sin,
but the righteous one sings and rejoices.

7 The righteous person knows the rights
of the poor,
but the wicked one does not understand
these concerns.

8 Mockers inflame a city,
but the wise turn away anger.

9 If a wise person goes to court with a fool,
there will be ranting and raving
but no resolution.

10 Bloodthirsty men hate an honest person,
but the upright care about him.

11 A fool gives full vent to his anger,
but a wise person holds it in check.

12 If a ruler listens to lies,
all his officials will be wicked.

13 The poor and the oppressor have this
in common:
the Lord gives light to the eyes of both.

14 A king who judges the poor
with fairness—
his throne will be established forever.

15 A rod of correction imparts wisdom,
but a youth left to himself
is a disgrace to his mother.

16 When the wicked increase,
rebellion increases,
but the righteous will see their downfall.

17 Discipline your child, and it will bring you
peace of mind
and give you delight.

18 Without revelation people run wild,
but one who follows divine instruction
will be happy.

19 A servant cannot be disciplined by words;
though he understands,
he doesn't respond.

20 Do you see someone who speaks
too soon?
There is more hope for a fool than for him.

21 A servant pampered from his youth
will become arrogant later on.

22 An angry person stirs up conflict,
and a hot-tempered one
increases rebellion.

23 A person's pride will humble him,
but a humble spirit will gain honor.

24 To be a thief's partner is to hate oneself;
he hears the curse but will not testify.

25 The fear of mankind is a snare,
but the one who trusts in the Lord
is protected.

26 Many desire a ruler's favor,
but a person receives justice
from the Lord.

27 An unjust person is detestable
to the righteous,
and one whose way is upright
is detestable to the wicked.

The Key to Walking in Wisdom

If you were to give a "State of My Life" address today, what would be the main takeaway? No matter the specifics, your address would reveal you're either pursuing God's wisdom and vision or your own. Proverbs 29 teaches us that the pursuit of God's wisdom brings happiness, but the pursuit of our own wisdom sends us off the rails (v. 18).

True happiness in life is only found within God's plan, which is given to us in God's Word. When we entrust ourselves to God's Word, then we will live out God's wisdom for our lives. Wisdom is not simply understanding God's ways; it seeks to act in obedience to those ways. God's direction won't often make sense if we're looking at it from a worldly perspective. However, as the prompting of His Spirit matches the truth of His Word, we must act in obedience.

All of life is to be submitted to God's direction. When we continue to refuse God's wisdom, we'll eventually find ourselves utterly helpless (v. 1). But "the one who trusts in the Lord is protected" (v. 25). That's the key to walking in wisdom, isn't it? When we trust God completely, we will choose to walk in His wisdom in all areas of our lives—in our friendships, work, financial decisions, conflicts, crises, marriages, parenting—all of it! And walking in God's wisdom impacts the state of our lives. It doesn't mean we won't face any difficulty, but in those difficulties we'll find rest and happiness in the Lord's everlasting protection.

Think back on the past year of your life. How have you seen the truth of Proverbs 29:18?

What is an area of life where you struggle to trust the Lord completely? What would change in your life this week if you began to trust the Lord completely in that area?

Trust God completely in all areas of your life.

THE WORDS OF AGUR

30 The words of Agur son of Jakeh.
The pronouncement.

The man's oration to Ithiel, to Ithiel
and Ucal:

2 I am more stupid than any other person,
and I lack a human's ability to understand.
3 I have not gained wisdom,
and I have no knowledge of the Holy One.
4 Who has gone up to heaven
and come down?
Who has gathered the wind in his hands?
Who has bound up the waters in a cloak?
Who has established all the ends
of the earth?
What is his name,
and what is the name of his son—
if you know?
5 Every word of God is pure;
he is a shield to those who take refuge
in him.
6 Don't add to his words,
or he will rebuke you, and you will be
proved a liar.

7 Two things I ask of you;
don't deny them to me before I die:
8 Keep falsehood and deceitful words
far from me.
Give me neither poverty nor wealth;
feed me with the food I need.
9 Otherwise, I might have too much
and deny you, saying, "Who is the LORD?"
or I might have nothing and steal,
profaning the name of my God.

10 Don't slander a servant to his master
or he will curse you, and you will
become guilty.

11 There is a generation that curses its father
and does not bless its mother.
12 There is a generation that is pure
in its own eyes,
yet is not washed from its filth.
13 There is a generation—how haughty
its eyes
and pretentious its looks.
14 There is a generation whose teeth
are swords,
whose fangs are knives,
devouring the oppressed from the land
and the needy from among mankind.

15 The leech has two daughters:
"Give, Give!"
Three things are never satisfied;
four never say, "Enough!":

16 Sheol; a childless womb;
earth, which is never satisfied with water;
and fire, which never says, "Enough!"

17 As for the eye that ridicules a father
and despises obedience to a mother,
may ravens of the valley pluck it out
and young vultures eat it.

18 Three things are too wondrous for me;
four I can't understand:
19 the way of an eagle in the sky,
the way of a snake on a rock,
the way of a ship at sea,
and the way of a man
with a young woman.

20 This is the way of an adulteress:
she eats and wipes her mouth
and says, "I've done nothing wrong."

21 The earth trembles under three things;
it cannot bear up under four:
22 a servant when he becomes king,
a fool when he is stuffed with food,
23 an unloved woman when she marries,
and a servant girl when she ousts
her queen.

24 Four things on earth are small,
yet they are extremely wise:
25 ants are not a strong people,
yet they store up their food
in the summer;
26 hyraxes are not a mighty people,
yet they make their homes in the cliffs;
27 locusts have no king,
yet all of them march in ranks;
28 a lizard can be caught in your hands,
yet it lives in kings' palaces.

29 Three things are stately in their stride;
four are stately in their walk:
30 a lion, which is mightiest among beasts
and doesn't retreat before anything;
31 a strutting rooster; a goat;
and a king at the head of his army.

32 If you have been foolish
by exalting yourself
or if you've been scheming,
put your hand over your mouth.
33 For the churning of milk produces butter,
and twisting a nose draws blood,
and stirring up anger produces strife.

Daily Pursuit and Refuge

The words of Agur that begin Proverbs 30 might seem strange in a book of wisdom. You don't expect a writer of wise proverbs to lack wisdom, much less to describe himself as "more stupid than any other person" (v. 2)! Agur's confession of ignorance here, however, helps make his point—God stands alone as the supreme source of truth. None of us can measure up, not even Solomon, Agur, or any other person who contributed to the pages of Scripture. In fact, human attempts to conceive and construct wisdom ultimately bring us to a place of deep and certain humility. None of us can fathom the depths of God's matchless wisdom (vv. 4-6).

As we come to the last two chapters of Proverbs, the heart behind Agur's words in verses 2-6 are essential if we are to continue receiving God's everlasting wisdom for everyday life. We do well to read and contemplate the Proverbs each day. At the same time, we must come to terms with this: the more we seek God's wisdom, the more we will realize we still don't know.

This is precisely why God's wisdom is a daily pursuit. God doesn't give us all His wisdom at the moment of salvation, once and for all time. As long as we live, we'll face new situations that will leave us feeling ignorant, just like Agur. As we study Proverbs, we won't somehow know God completely and have all the answers. What we can know, though, is that the wisdom we need every day originates with God who loves us and wants to show us the way. And He will—as we trust Him and take refuge in the truth of His timeless Word.

What is a situation where you have been tempted to add human "wisdom" instead of trusting completely in the wisdom of God's Word (v. 6)? Why?

What does it mean that "every word of God is pure" (v. 5)? How does this fact speak to you about daily situations where you might feel ignorant (v. 2)?

None of us can fathom the depths of God's matchless wisdom.

MONTH	DAY	YEAR
. .	. .	. .

THE WORDS OF LEMUEL

31 The words of King Lemuel,
a pronouncement that his mother
taught him:

2 What should I say, my son?
What, son of my womb?
What, son of my vows?

3 Don't spend your energy on women
or your efforts on those
who destroy kings.

4 It is not for kings, Lemuel,
it is not for kings to drink wine
or for rulers to desire beer.

5 Otherwise, he will drink,
forget what is decreed,
and pervert justice for all
the oppressed.

6 Give beer to one who is dying
and wine to one whose life is bitter.

7 Let him drink so that he can forget
his poverty
and remember his trouble no more.

8 Speak up for those who have
no voice,
for the justice of all
who are dispossessed.

9 Speak up, judge righteously,
and defend the cause of
the oppressed and needy.

IN PRAISE OF A WIFE OF NOBLE CHARACTER

10 Who can find a wife
of noble character?
She is far more precious than jewels.

11 The heart of her husband trusts
in her,
and he will not lack anything good.

12 She rewards him with good, not evil,
all the days of her life.

13 She selects wool and flax
and works with willing hands.

14 She is like the merchant ships,
bringing her food from far away.

15 She rises while it is still night
and provides food for her household
and portions for her female servants.

16 She evaluates a field and buys it;
she plants a vineyard
with her earnings.

17 She draws on her strength
and reveals that her arms are strong.

18 She sees that her profits are good,
and her lamp never goes out at night.

19 She extends her hands
to the spinning staff,
and her hands hold the spindle.

20 Her hands reach out to the poor,
and she extends her hands
to the needy.

21 She is not afraid for her household
when it snows,
for all in her household
are doubly clothed.

22 She makes her own bed coverings;
her clothing is fine linen and purple.

23 Her husband is known
at the city gates,
where he sits among the elders
of the land.

24 She makes and sells linen garments;
she delivers belts to the merchants.

25 Strength and honor are her clothing,
and she can laugh at the time
to come.

26 Her mouth speaks wisdom,
and loving instruction is
on her tongue.

27 She watches over the activities
of her household
and is never idle.

28 Her children rise up
and call her blessed;
her husband also praises her:

29 "Many women have done
noble deeds,
but you surpass them all!"

30 Charm is deceptive and beauty
is fleeting,
but a woman who fears the LORD
will be praised.

31 Give her the reward of her labor,
and let her works praise her
at the city gates.

Laying Groundwork for the Future

Throughout the book of Proverbs, we've learned the effects of walking in God's wisdom. In the final chapter of the book, we're given a portrait of a person who chooses that path as a lifestyle. The woman described is fierce—caring for her family, caring for the poor, working outside the home, buying property, cultivating the land, and more. She is strong, discerning, committed, and caring. Her example might seem out of reach, but the essence of it all is that she daily chooses to walk with God in His wisdom. In the end, other people can't help but recognize the legacy of godly wisdom she leaves, and celebrate that legacy.

What a blessing it would be for others to see all the ways that Jesus works in and through us. This isn't to earn spiritual "brownie points," take the credit for what the Spirit does, or even for the sake of attaining some measure of earthly legacy, in and of itself. But it does remind us that our lives are meant to be multiplied. Whether we have children of our own or we raise and invest in the spiritual family that God provides, we are meant to multiply our lives in the next generation.

To do that, we need wisdom that we don't possess in our flesh. We need the Lord to give us words of wisdom in our conversations. We need Him to transform our thoughts and attitudes. We need Him to move us and motivate us for His kingdom work—work that starts in our own homes. Those things are only possible when we are anchored in God's Word and obedient to His Spirit within us.

We are laying spiritual groundwork for the future in the ways that we choose to walk in God's wisdom today. This is where our legacies are forged. As we seek God's everlasting wisdom for everyday life, we leave a legacy that far outlives us.

How would you summarize the wisdom presented in the woman of Proverbs 31?

In practical terms, what steps can you begin to take now to pass on a legacy of wisdom to those who come behind you?

Everlasting wisdom lived out in everyday life leaves a legacy.

Get the most from your study.

The book of Proverbs explores important themes, such as humility, hard work, wealth, relationships, and leadership. Through this study and regular Bible reading, you will receive wisdom directly from the source of all wisdom and enjoy the benefits of applying it to your circumstances.

In this study you'll:

- Learn how to understand and interpret proverbs
- Develop the spiritual discipline of daily Bible reading
- Distinguish worldly wisdom from godly wisdom
- Begin making decisions informed by the Scriptures

To enrich your study experience, take advantage of the *Proverbs* videos from author Vance Pitman.

STUDYING ON YOUR OWN?

Remember to watch the daily teaching sessions available through the redemption code printed in this *Bible Study Book*.

LEADING A GROUP?

Each group member will need a *Proverbs Bible Study Book*, which includes access to the four session videos. Because all participants will have access to the video content, you can choose to watch the videos outside of your group meeting if desired. Or, if you're watching together and someone misses a group meeting, they'll have the flexibility to catch up!

ADDITIONAL RESOURCES

eBOOK
Includes the content of this printed book but offers the convenience and flexibility that come with mobile technology.

005839201 **$16.99**

More *Proverbs* resources can be found online at lifeway.com/proverbs

Price and availability subject to change without notice.

PROVERBS

Everlasting Wisdom for Everyday Life

Here's Your Video Access

To stream the Bible study teaching videos, follow these steps:

1. Go to my.lifeway.com/redeem and register or log in to your Lifeway account.

2. Enter this redemption code to gain access to your individual-use video license:

CKQ1QLJJY1

Once you've entered your personal redemption code, you can stream the Bible study teaching videos any time from your Digital Media page on my.lifeway.com or watch them via the Lifeway On Demand app on a compatible TV or mobile device via your Lifeway account.

There's no need to enter your code more than once! To watch your streaming videos, just log in to your Lifeway account at my.lifeway.com or watch using the Lifeway On Demand app.

QUESTIONS? WE HAVE ANSWERS!
Visit support.lifeway.com and search "Video Redemption Code" or "Video Streaming FAQ" or call our Tech Support Team at 866.627.8553.